THE BEDFORD SERIES IN HISTORY AND CULTURE

Jerry Falwell and the Rise of the Religious Right

A Brief History with Documents

Falwell and the Rise of the Religious Right

A Brief History with Documents

Matthew Avery Sutton

Washington State University

BEDFORD / ST. MARTIN'S   Boston ◆ New York

For Bedford/St. Martin's

Publisher for History: Mary V. Dougherty
Senior Executive Editor for History: William J. Lombardo
Director of Development for History: Jane Knetzger
Senior Editor: Heidi L. Hood
Developmental Editor: Michelle McSweeney
Production Supervisor: Victoria Sharoyan
Senior Marketing Manager for U.S. History: Amy Whitaker
Editorial Assistant: Laura Kintz
Project Management: Books By Design, Inc.
Permissions Manager: Kalina K. Ingham
Text Designer: Claire Seng-Niemoeller
Cover Designer: Marine Miller
Cover Photo: Mark Meyer/Time Life Pictures/Getty Images
Composition: Achorn International, Inc.
Printing and Binding: RR Donnelley and Sons

President, Bedford/St. Martin's: Denise B. Wydra
Presidents, Macmillan Higher Education: Joan E. Feinberg and Tom Scotty
Director of Marketing: Karen R. Soeltz
Production Director: Susan W. Brown
Associate Production Director: Elise S. Kaiser
Manager, Publishing Services: Andrea Cava

Library of Congress Control Number: 2012942564

Manufactured in the United States of America.

7   6   5   4   3   2
f   e   d   c   b   a

For information, write: Bedford/St. Martin's, 75 Arlington Street, Boston, MA 02116
(617-399-4000)

ISBN: 978-1-4576-1110-0

Acknowledgments

Foreword

The Bedford Series in History and Culture is designed so that readers can study the past as historians do.

The historian's first task is finding the evidence. Documents, letters, memoirs, interviews, pictures, movies, novels, or poems can provide facts and clues. Then the historian questions and compares the sources. There is more to do than in a courtroom, for hearsay evidence is welcome, and the historian is usually looking for answers beyond act and motive. Different views of an event may be as important as a single verdict. How a story is told may yield as much information as what it says.

Along the way the historian seeks help from other historians and perhaps from specialists in other disciplines. Finally, it is time to write, to decide on an interpretation and how to arrange the evidence for readers.

Each book in this series contains an important historical document or group of documents, each document a witness from the past and open to interpretation in different ways. The documents are combined with some element of historical narrative—an introduction or a biographical essay, for example—that provides students with an analysis of the primary source material and important background information about the world in which it was produced.

Each book in the series focuses on a specific topic within a specific historical period. Each provides a basis for lively thought and discussion about several aspects of the topic and the historian's role. Each is short enough (and inexpensive enough) to be a reasonable one-week assignment in a college course. Whether as classroom or personal reading, each book in the series provides firsthand experience of the challenge—and fun—of discovering, recreating, and interpreting the past.

Lynn Hunt
David W. Blight
Bonnie G. Smith
Natalie Zemon Davis

To Jackson and Nathan

Preface

Shortly before Reverend Jerry Falwell died in 2007, he told National Public Radio's Steve Inskeep, "A pastor has to be media-savvy if he's going to reach everybody. I don't mean to be ugly and harsh, but to be forthright and candid. And the result is that people that don't like you start listening."[1] The man from Lynchburg, Virginia, was one of the most media-savvy U.S. ministers ever. Whether people perceived him as ugly and harsh or as forthright and candid, they listened. And they did much more than that: they acted. Together, Falwell and his followers redefined politics and culture in the United States.

Jerry Falwell and the Rise of the Religious Right focuses on the ways in which the political mobilization of large numbers of theologically conservative Protestants—along with a handful of Catholics—revitalized American conservatism, gave birth to the modern Religious Right, and reshaped the Republican Party in the 1970s and early 1980s. In particular, it analyzes the successful deployment of religion for explicitly partisan purposes. Ultimately this book will help today's students—most of whom were born after the launch of the culture wars—make sense of the ways that politicized religion has affected the world they have inherited.

Few modern American leaders have been as important or as controversial as Jerry Falwell (1933–2007). His life and work touch on almost all of the major issues of the 1970s and 1980s, including the cold war, changing gender roles, civil rights, the politicalization of evangelicalism, the regeneration of modern conservatism, and the Reagan Revolution. This book is not about Falwell for his own sake; instead it uses his life as a lens into major cultural shifts. It is designed for courses in modern United States history and the introductory survey course as well as more specialized courses in American politics or religion.

---

[1]Steve Inskeep,"Religion, Politics a Potent Mix for Jerry Falwell," National Public Radio, *Morning Edition*, June 30, 2006 (www.npr.org/templates/story/story .php?storyId=5522064).

The introductory essay in Part One encourages students to think about the ways in which the life of Jerry Falwell touches on and reflects the ebbs and flows of modern U.S. history and the rise of the Religious Right. By focusing on an individual rather than on the larger movement, the introduction allows students to gain insights into major issues and themes in a specific and accessible way. It also helps them see that culture wars are never only about abstract ideas or debates, but are always about real lives and real people. Through this framework, the introduction outlines the emergence of modern evangelicalism and the reaction of conservative Christians to the teaching of evolution and decline of prayer in schools, the cold war, desegregation, abortion, gay rights, and other social movements, as well the role of the Religious Right in the politics of the 1970s and 1980s.

The documents in Part Two illuminate the issues that helped shape Falwell's work. They focus on significant social concerns that came to define the culture wars and the modern Religious Right. Most of them originally appeared in the 1970s and 1980s. Although numerous historians (including me) have identified roots of the Religious Right in much earlier periods, this book is not as much concerned with the movement's foundations or its post-Reagan reincarnations as with its emergence in the 1970s and 1980s as a visible, powerful political force.

The lively and engaging documents, which are certain to provoke student discussion and analysis, have been arranged in thematic sections. The first section focuses on the issues and ideas that characterized post–World War II evangelicalism in some of its many forms. The second section explores the role of race in pushing conservative Christians to think about their standing in American society. The third section looks at education and evangelicals' concerns that public schools had become hostile to people of faith. The fourth section focuses on the most controversial issues of the period for evangelicals and their allies—those related to family, including gender roles, abortion, and homosexuality. The final section makes explicit what had been implicit in the previous sections—that evangelicals in the 1970s and 1980s found a long-term home in the Republican Party.

To help students get the most from this volume, the documents are followed by a chronology, questions for consideration, and a selected bibliography.

A NOTE ABOUT THE TEXT

I spend little time in this book discussing the differences among the various evangelical subgroups that constituted the Religious Right in the post–World War II era. While there were important distinctions between those who, for example, described themselves as "fundamentalists" and those who claimed the title of "new-evangelicals," by the last decades of the twentieth century all but the most hard-core fundamentalists had put aside their differences with more moderate pentecostals and new-evangelicals to work for the cause of a more "Christian" America. Because Falwell was particularly instrumental in rendering the fundamentalist-evangelical distinction almost meaningless, especially in the arena of politics, I use the term *evangelical* broadly in reference to both politically active fundamentalists and the many groups who identified with the new-evangelical movement.

For readability, obvious typos in original documents have been silently corrected; grammatical errors and other inconsistencies in language and style have been left as is.

ACKNOWLEDGMENTS

I am grateful to many friends and scholars for their help on this book. Jane Sherron De Hart of the University of California, Santa Barbara, has been an ideal mentor for more than a decade. Senior Executive Editor William Lombardo at Bedford/St. Martin's supported this book from the beginning and offered many excellent suggestions. My agent, Sandra Dijkstra, helped me make it a reality. Several colleagues and reviewers offered numerous ideas for the book, including Michael S. Hamilton, Seattle Pacific University; Paul Harvey, University of Colorado, Colorado Springs; Malcolm D. Magee, Michigan State University; Steven P. Miller, Webster University; Andrew S. Moore, Saint Anselm University; David Sehat, Georgia State University; John G. Turner, George Mason University; and David Harrington Watt, Temple University. Seth Dowland, Pacific Lutheran University; Paul Ericksen, director of the Billy Graham Center Archives; Patrick Robbins, Bob Jones University archivist; and Daniel K. Williams, University of West Georgia, generously provided both ideas and hard-to-locate documents. The staff at Bedford/St. Martin's, including Heidi Hood and Laura Kintz, along with freelance editor Michelle McSweeney, has been a dream to work with. Andrea Cava at Bedford/St. Martin's and Nancy Benjamin at Books By Design managed the production of the book with great skill. My parents, John and Kathy Sutton, have encouraged me in all that I do and have endured many discussions about the issues included in this book. My wife, Kristen—a "total woman" of a different kind—has enthusiastically supported my passion for all things religious, political, and historical. For her love, I am forever grateful. I dedicate this book to our boys, Jackson and Nathan. They provide the best imaginable distraction from work. I hope that the culture wars of my generation will truly be history by the time they are old enough to read these pages.

Matthew Avery Sutton

Contents

5. God and the GOP 119

APPENDIXES

Illustrations

Introduction: Evangelicals and the Reconstruction of American Politics and Culture

As the 1980 presidential campaign heated up, Republican nominee Ronald Reagan attended a revival meeting in Dallas, Texas, where he addressed an enthusiastic crowd of fifteen thousand flag-waving, Bible-carrying Christians. "I know you can't endorse me," he began. "But I want you to know I endorse you and what you are doing." Cheers rang out. Reagan praised the crowd for bringing "a new vitality" to American politics and, echoing their ideals, affirmed that the Bible was indeed the solution to the world's problems. "Religious America is awakening," he concluded, "perhaps just in time for our country's sake."[1]

The *New York Times* headline perfectly summed up the meeting: "Reagan Backs Evangelicals in Their Political Activities." What the *Times* coverage of this event ignored, however, was the decades of hard work across multiple generations that had laid the foundations for this meeting. For years evangelical leaders, conservative businessmen, and political activists had built relationships and traded ideas. But they had not organized, at least not until the late 1970s. The student revolutions, the second wave of feminism, the civil and gay rights movements, the national nightmare of Watergate, and the seeming loss of American prestige in the Vietnam War pushed many evangelicals to take politics more seriously. They believed that their nation was moving away from its Christian foundations. Realizing that evangelicals constituted one of the country's largest untapped voting blocs, conservative political

1

strategists sensed an opportunity. As a result, they targeted a handful of celebrity ministers for recruitment. They knew that if they could convert the ministers to their causes, the ministers—using their influence and their extensive media empires—could shift the balance of power in the country to the right. Meanwhile, at the grassroots level, thousands of Christian activists worked in communities around the country to integrate better their faith with their politics. Ultimately, these men and women, along with their media-savvy preachers, transformed the Republican Party and with it the trajectory of the nation.

The evangelicals who rallied behind Reagan in Texas constituted a diverse group. Broadly defined, evangelicals are theologically conservative Protestants who emphasize the authority of the Bible, the death and resurrection of Jesus, the necessity of individual conversion, and the spreading of the faith through missions. Evangelicalism encompasses many different subgroups ranging, for example, from tongues-speaking pentecostals to ultraconservative fundamentalists. However, the nuances that distinguish the millions of people who identify as evangelicals matter little in the contemporary political realm. Regardless of the theological diversity within evangelicalism, a substantial number of evangelicals from many different denominations and sects have united in recent decades to create an identifiable political movement that has transformed modern America.

Many men and women helped shape modern American evangelicalism. From Billy Sunday in the 1910s to Aimee Semple McPherson in the 1930s to Billy Graham in the 1950s to Francis Schaeffer in the 1970s, religious leaders across the twentieth century have inspired their followers to work for the redemption of American culture. Perhaps the most colorful and controversial leader in recent years has been Jerry Falwell, who by helping mold evangelicals into one of the most powerful voting blocs in the nation contributed to the so-called Reagan Revolution and the rebirth of American conservatism. Part I of this book focuses largely on Falwell, but it is about much more than one person. Falwell's life provides a lens into the issues and concerns expressed in the documents in Part II that mobilized millions of conservative Christians to organize what eventually became the Religious Right.

MAKING JERRY FALWELL

Jerry Falwell was born in Lynchburg, Virginia, on August 11, 1933. His mother, Helen, came from a long line of proud Baptists. The Bible, prayer, and the church served as the pillars of her life. She raised her children in the faith, hoping to instill her beliefs in them. Falwell's father, Carey, was an entrepreneur, a thriving bootleg-liquor distributor during Prohibition, and a successful businessman. Unlike his wife, Carey had little tolerance for religion. He was an avowed agnostic who hated preachers. Nevertheless, he allowed his children to go to church with their mother.

Lynchburg's public schools reinforced Helen's religious efforts. As Jerry wistfully remembered, teachers and principals worked to shape and mold the character of their students by training them in the Christian faith. Falwell attended weekly chapel services, memorized scripture, and recited the Lord's Prayer before classes. But for him, religion just didn't take. Although his mother ushered him to Sunday school every weekend, he snuck out as often as he could.

Falwell graduated from high school in 1950, leaving his mark as a popular athlete with excellent grades. He was a practical joker, too. He once wrestled an overbearing physical education teacher to the floor during class and stole his britches, promptly tacking them on the school bulletin board. On another occasion he locked a math teacher in a closet to avoid a quiz, and he terrorized his Latin teacher by hiding a rat in her snack drawer. Despite achieving valedictorian honors, Falwell was not allowed to give a speech at graduation as punishment for his pranks. While Falwell made light of his past, critics of the minister see in these examples Jerry's propensity to bully those he disliked.

Falwell enrolled in college immediately after high school. He registered as a pre-mechanical engineering student at Lynchburg College, a local Christian school. Despite the required courses in Bible and theology, he showed little interest in spiritual matters. He remembered his second year on campus, 1951–1952, as a year of "panty raids, flying-saucer stories, and 'Ike for President' rallies."[2]

Falwell enthusiastically supported Republican candidate and war hero Dwight D. Eisenhower over Adlai Stevenson for president in 1952. Virginians, like most citizens of the former Confederacy, had overwhelmingly supported Democrats since the Civil War, demonstrating their loyalty to the party that defended state's rights (and racial segregation) against the power of the federal government. However, during the 1930s, the Democratic Party under Franklin Roosevelt began to evolve. Roosevelt believed that the supposed "invisible hand" of the market could no longer guarantee individual liberties and freedoms in a world characterized by behemoth corporations, extreme inequalities of wealth, an economic depression at home, and the threat of fascism and totalitarianism abroad. He called for a more active, more responsive federal government that would protect and guarantee the liberties of individuals in the face of these unprecedented challenges and built a new political coalition that brought together progressives, blue-collar workers, urban Americans, farmers, and immigrants. He also did his best to hold onto the "solid" South, but white southern Democrats grew increasingly leery of the expanding New Deal state during the 1930s. By the early 1950s, the old South's loyalty to the party of Andrew Jackson was fading. In fact, Virginia was one of several southern states that voted Republican in the 1952 presidential race.

Politics was not the most important thing in Falwell's life that year. On what started off as a routine Sunday morning, he awoke to the enticing smell of hoecakes and bacon wafting up the stairs of his mother's house along with the sounds of her radio tuned to Charles Fuller's *Old Fashioned Revival Hour*. Fuller was one of the pioneers of Christian media who by the mid-1940s had an audience estimated at 20 million. A typical broadcast included upbeat hymns, his wife's reading of inspirational letters from listeners, and a short sermon on one or more of the fundamentals of the Christian faith that Charles delivered in simple, plain language. His program succeeded by blending the best of the nineteenth-century evangelical revival tradition with the latest twentieth-century technology.

If Jerry wanted to eat a good, home-cooked breakfast complete with fresh molasses syrup, he had to stomach the Fullers at the breakfast table. It was a worthwhile tradeoff. As he later recalled, he "entered the kitchen a playful penitent entering the skid-row mission, willing to listen to the chaplain's sermon in exchange for a hot homemade breakfast." But something was different that day. As he listened to the radio, he felt a lump growing in his throat. Soon he felt like crying. He could not identify what was happening in his life. That afternoon, he surprised his "gang" of friends by asking if any of them knew of a church in town that preached the same message as Fuller. Although the group assumed that Jerry was setting them up for some kind of joke, a couple of guys told him about Park Avenue Baptist Church. That night, at the end of the service, eighteen-year-old Jerry Falwell accepted the minister's invitation to come to the altar. There he kneeled, confessed that he was a sinner, asked Jesus Christ to enter his life, and prayed to be born again. "From that moment," he recalled, "everything changed for me."[3]

A couple of intense months later, Falwell decided to dedicate his life to full-time Christian ministry. He found the right school to nurture his beliefs and his vision for the future in Baptist Bible College (BBC) in Springfield, Missouri, where he joined the increasing number of other

Christians who were matriculating at fundamentalist-oriented Bible schools in the mid-twentieth century.[4]

THE ORIGINS OF AMERICAN FUNDAMENTALISM

At Baptist Bible College, Falwell entered the mainstream of the American fundamentalist movement. Hailing from many different denominations, fundamentalists were conservative evangelicals who in the first decades of the twentieth century called for a return to what they defined as the "fundamentals" of the Christian faith. In the context of massive urbanization, the popularization of Darwinian evolution, the increasing prominence of literary-critical approaches to the Bible, significant Catholic and Jewish immigration, and the systematic study of world religions that undermined Christian distinctiveness, many evangelicals determined that the world was careening toward the apocalypse. True Christianity, they believed, was under siege, and they went to war for the authentic faith.

Before long a network of many of the nation's most important white evangelical ministers, radio personalities, missionaries, evangelists, publishers, and Bible college teachers coalesced into a definable movement that adopted the name "fundamentalism." They promoted individual salvation, the authority of the Bible, and the imminent second coming of Christ. They were characterized as much by what they opposed as by what they advocated. They waged a public battle against liberal theology—called "modernism"—and what they interpreted as its many political, cultural, and theological consequences, which ranged from declining morals to women's popular clothing styles. As Falwell famously quipped, "a fundamentalist is an evangelical who is mad about something." While African American churches wrestled with some of the same issues and challenges, white fundamentalists did not welcome black evangelicals into the fundamentalist coalition.

In the 1910s fundamentalists became increasingly anxious about the trajectory of the nation, and tensions with liberal Protestants escalated. By the outbreak of World War I, what had started as a fairly abstract intellectual debate over definitions of the "true faith" turned explosive. While modernists worked to reform society and struggled alongside President Woodrow Wilson to "make the world safe for democracy," most fundamentalists warned that the apocalypse was imminent and that spiritual salvation was humans' only hope. Each side accused the other of abandoning the true faith. Battle lines were drawn, and both groups made it their mission to purge the other from mainstream Protestant institutions.

The fundamentalist-modernist controversy raged within the nation's churches through the 1920s and 1930s. Eventually, the liberals emerged victorious, securing control of most of the mainstream denominations and the nation's most influential theological schools and seminaries. The fundamentalists took rejection as another sign that the return of Jesus was imminent, and they ultimately had the last laugh. In the 1930s the power of mainline denominations began to plateau, and the popularity of fundamentalism simultaneously surged. Although it would not be apparent for decades, the years of the Great Depression marked the beginning of the decline of the old-line Protestant denominations and the beginning of evangelical dominance in the United States.

Defeating theological liberalism was never fundamentalists' only concern. During the 1920s, fundamentalists and their like-minded allies across the country worked to pass laws eliminating what they considered the blasphemous teaching of Darwin's theory of evolution from public schools. They were successful in Tennessee, provoking the ire of the American Civil Liberties Union (ACLU), a recently founded civil rights organization. Seeking to challenge Tennessee's anti-evolution ban, the ACLU hired prominent attorney Clarence Darrow to defend John Scopes, a local biology teacher who had agreed to serve as the defendant in a test case. The prosecution recruited famed orator, politician, and former secretary of state William Jennings Bryan to serve as its counsel. In a highly publicized trial, the judge convicted Scopes of violating the law. This was a victory for fundamentalism, but much of the national media condescendingly depicted fundamentalists as stereotypical rural, southern, anti-intellectuals. As fundamentalists and other evangelicals continued to battle the teaching of evolution in the schools in the second half of the twentieth century, the negative associations that grew out of the *Scopes* trial haunted them.

REMAKING AMERICAN EVANGELICALISM

During the interwar era, fundamentalists developed new strategies for working outside the traditional spheres of religious power. They started new churches, schools, colleges, and independent denominations. But they also increasingly witnessed the unanticipated consequences of having lost control of the nation's established denominations. In particular, they realized that the federal government, the country's most influential journalists, and the large radio networks all had relationships with established Protestant groups. In forsaking traditional denominations, fundamentalists ceded their ability to speak to those in power on behalf of U.S. religious communities. They needed to organize in order to regain some of their lost influence. To that end, the most powerful and influential white fundamentalists in the nation established the National Association of Evangelicals for United Action (NAE) in 1942. Its purpose, as founder Ralph T. Davis explained in a letter to fundamentalist minister William Bell Riley, was to find "some common meeting ground for representation to government where legal matters may be handled as they concern one endeavor or another of the evangelical forces." Riley agreed, persuaded that a new organization was needed to exercise "righteous influence in government affairs."[5]

NAE leaders also agreed that it was time for a slight modification of their identity. The term *fundamentalist*, especially in the wake of the *Scopes* trial, invoked images of dogmatic, close-minded, reactionary religious fanatics. The men who founded the NAE hoped to engage seriously with the broader culture so as to have the best opportunity to reshape it along Christian lines. They clung tenaciously to the fundamentals, but they took a more positive and affirming approach to relating with the outside world. They settled on the name "new evangelical" to describe their movement, later shortening it to the historic term *evangelical* (Document 1).

The evangelicals' most famous representative in the post–World War II era was Billy Graham. Born in 1918 in North Carolina, Graham spent the late 1940s working as an evangelist for a national Christian youth ministry. By the end of the decade, he was holding revivals in the nation's biggest cities. During the 1950s, he perfected his folksy, down-home style and preached to some of the largest audiences ever assembled for religious meetings. His message was simple: All people are separated from God because of their sins, but if they accept Jesus into their hearts, he will forgive them and reconcile them to God, ensuring that they spend eternity in heaven. Behind this simple message was an extremely sophisticated mass media empire that Graham built on radio, television, film, magazines, and best-selling books. He also helped found *Christianity Today* in 1956, a magazine that has defined the parameters of modern evangelicalism ever since. Meanwhile, Graham's strident anticommunism and his influence over millions of Americans in the hyper-religious cold war context gave him entrée into the world of elite politics. Beginning with Harry Truman, he advised every president up to and including Barack Obama. While he claimed that his work was nonpartisan, he nudged conservative Christians to the political right, helping establish the context from which the Religious Right would later emerge (Document 2).[6]

Not all fundamentalists in the 1940s embraced the open and culture-affirming approach that Graham and the NAE were promoting. Some clung tenaciously to the label "fundamentalist." Conservative firebrand Carl McIntire, for example, created the American Council of Christian Churches in 1941 to unify fundamentalists. He called for strict separation from mainstream culture (which was always easier said than done) and for hard-line, uncompromising positions. He represented the far right of the fundamentalist movement in an era in which most leaders were moving toward the center in an effort to reengage with the broader culture and to find like-minded allies. This tradition of militant fundamentalist separatism attracted Falwell and shaped both the church where he converted and Baptist Bible College. Eventually, however, Falwell grew more moderate, helping build bridges between fundamentalists and new evangelicals. By the time he organized the Moral Majority in 1979, the distinction between "fundamentalist" and "evangelical" was almost meaningless, especially in terms of politics.

Falwell arrived at BBC in 1952, driving a decade-old Plymouth that proudly sported an "Ike for President" bumper sticker. The school was an offshoot of the work of one of the more famous preachers of the 1920s and 1930s, J. Frank Norris. Known as the "Texas Tornado," Norris was a staunch critic of liberal theology. He was also an institution builder, founding multiple churches, periodicals, and Bible institutes. He was famous in part because of his speaking skills. But he had also gained national notoriety in 1926 when he shot and killed an unarmed man in his church office (he claimed self-defense and was acquitted). Even when he wasn't packing heat, Norris could be difficult to work with, and in 1950 a handful of leaders from his church and seminary left to found a new conservative denomination, Baptist Bible Fellowship, and a school, Baptist Bible College.

Falwell's time at BBC coincided with U.S. engagement in an increasingly serious cold war. President Truman believed that the United States had a divine calling to oppose the Soviet Union. For American leaders and policymakers, communism's explicit atheism made the battle about more than competing economic systems. They drew on religion as a source of inspiration and saturated their speeches with biblical rhetoric. Truman's successor, President Eisenhower, masterfully linked the cold

The Preacher
A young Jerry Falwell preaching at the Thomas Road Baptist Church,
ca. early 1970s.

war to issues of religion. In 1954 he famously declared, "Our government makes no sense unless it is founded on a deeply felt religious faith—and I don't care what it is." Such claims tapped into a deep American tradition of civil religion that dated back to the Puritans. Many Americans believed that the United States—like ancient Israel—had been divinely chosen by God to play a major part in his plan for the ongoing redemption of the world. They believed that the United States was destined to bring God's message (economic, political, and religious) to the rest of the world. Such an ideology melded perfectly with the cold war. Congress's addition of the phrase "under God" to the Pledge of Allegiance in 1954 (to distinguish it from so-called atheist pledges of communist countries) and its 1956 elevation of "In God We Trust" to the national motto further demonstrated the hold of civil religion on the American consciousness in this period.

Like millions of other Americans, Falwell embraced the cold war vision that linked God and country. During the 1950s, attendance at the nation's churches and synagogues skyrocketed, enrollment at seminaries surged, and construction of new houses of worship boomed. However, Falwell's home church, Park Avenue Baptist, was struggling. The church had hired a new pastor, and, as is often the case, some members had trouble adjusting to the new leadership. By the time Falwell returned from school in 1956, some of the most prominent members of the congregation, including the family of his girlfriend Macel Pate, decided to start a new church. They asked the twenty-two-year-old Falwell to serve as their pastor. He agreed. The congregation held its first service on June 21, 1956, in an abandoned Donald Duck soda bottling plant, which served as a makeshift sanctuary.

Falwell immediately started to build the new church, Thomas Road Baptist, by visiting everyone in the neighborhood and inviting them to Sunday services. He also turned to the radio for additional publicity. He had been raised on the *Old Fashioned Revival Hour* and the radio sermons of southern evangelist Bob Jones (founder of Bob Jones University), and he wanted to follow in the footsteps of his heroes. When a new country-and-western music station began broadcasting in Lynchburg, he bought airtime—a half-hour slot each morning—from the owner. The ambitious young minister used those thirty minutes to preach, tell stories of faith, and promote the Thomas Road church.

Falwell next bought a half-hour of airtime each week from the local ABC television affiliate and started a new program. Like many of his most successful peers, he quickly recognized the tremendous potential of new mass media for spreading the Christian faith. "No other preachers were on television then," he recalled. "Television made me a kind of instant celebrity." By the time the church celebrated its first anniversary in 1957, it boasted a radio program, a TV ministry, and regular Sunday attendance numbering in the hundreds. The church soon expanded its mission by opening a home for recovering alcoholics (inspired at least in part by Falwell's memory of his father's struggles with alcohol) and eventually an urban ministry for the poor. In 1967 Falwell founded Lynchburg Christian Academy, a school for kindergarten through high school students. He had married Macel Pate in 1958, and together they were raising a growing family. By the late 1960s more than two thousand people worshipped at Thomas Road Baptist Church each Sunday.[7]

Falwell dreamed bigger still. He embarked on a new venture, this time in the world of higher education. He established Liberty University, which he hoped to build into the largest and best Christian liberal arts university in the nation, a school that would garner national respect for fundamentalists and train the best and brightest in the movement.[8]

Falwell's interest in Christian education at the secondary and college levels grew out of his frustration with the direction of American public education. The inclusion of Darwinian evolution in science classes had rankled evangelicals since the *Scopes* trial in the 1920s. In the early 1960s U.S. Supreme Court rulings against officially sanctioned prayer and Bible reading in public schools further outraged the faithful (Document 11). More and more schools were including sex education in their curricula (Document 12). With God out and sex in, conservative Protestants believed that attendance in public schools put their children at risk, and many ministers joined Falwell in creating Christian alternative schools that taught evangelical-centered interpretations of history, science, and other subjects (Documents 13, 14, 15).

RACE AND THE POLITICALIZATION OF AMERICAN EVANGELICALS

During the 1960s and early 1970s, Falwell claimed that he had little interest in politics. However, like most conservative evangelicals (whether they identified as fundamentalists, pentecostals, or new evangelicals), he supported conservative causes and voted along conservative lines. He and his coreligionists believed that maintaining the cold war status quo reflected their biblical obligation to act as good citizens. They viewed supporting progressive or liberal causes as overreaching into "politics." Whether he was or was not interested in politics, politics soon became something that he could not ignore.

Typical of most southern evangelicals (Document 6), Falwell had grown up oblivious to the effects of racial segregation. Reflecting on this later in life, he wrote "in all those years it didn't cross my mind that segregation and its consequences for the human family were evil. I was blind to that reality." In fact, he supported the South's autonomy when it came to issues of race. In 1964 President Lyndon Johnson asked clergy across the nation to support the new civil rights bill. Falwell, like many other socially conservative ministers, including the feisty Carl McIntire (Document 7), did not give the president his endorsement. "It is a terrible violation of human and private property rights," Falwell claimed. "It should be considered civil wrongs rather than civil rights." The next year, in March 1965, Falwell preached one of the most famous (or infamous) sermons of his career in response to Reverend Martin Luther King Jr.'s famous march in Selma, Alabama. He began by reminding the men and women at Thomas Road Baptist Church that their citizenship resided in heaven, not on earth. "Preachers," he declared, "are not called to be politicians but to be soul winners. . . . If as much effort could be put into winning people to Jesus Christ across the land as is being exerted in the present civil rights movement, America would be turned upside down for God" (Document 8).[9]

That July three white and one black activist affiliated with the Congress for Racial Equality singled out the Thomas Road church for a protest. The minister's opposition to the civil rights movement had earned him national scorn. At the time Falwell joked that all the protesters needed was a good haircut. Years later, however, he admitted that they had displayed true courage. But Falwell maintained to the end of his life that movement activists had no impact on his views on race and justice. Articulating the typical evangelical position that God alone — not government, not laws, not the courts — can bring about true positive social change, he claimed that only the Almighty's voice on his heart had transformed him.

But others played significant roles as well. At about the same time that Martin Luther King Jr. was making headlines, Falwell's shoe-shine man, an elderly African American, asked the preacher when he would be allowed to join Thomas Road. Falwell, momentarily stunned and embarrassed, had no response. As Falwell navigated the issues of race in this period, he caught hell from every side. Local civil rights activists criticized him for supporting segregation, and with every tiny step he took toward inclusion, he lost white church members and their donations. He shamefully admitted years later that not until the end of the turbulent 1960s did he finally admit a black family into membership.

Falwell's views on race and politics surfaced again in 1968, when he opened his pulpit to George Wallace, who was running for president. A well-known segregationist who fought the intrusion of the federal government into the states and local communities, Wallace campaigned on a platform of "law and order" that appealed to working-class whites. Inviting Wallace to Thomas Road in the midst of a political campaign belied Falwell's claim that politics did not interest him.

Falwell's politicalization was further accelerated by a conflict with the federal government. The minister understood that in order to build Liberty into a truly first-class university and to keep up with his expanding congregation and multitude of ministries, he needed land, and a lot of it. In the early seventies he bought over two thousand acres on nearby Candler's Mountain (where Thomas Road Baptist Church and Liberty University are now located). To pay for the expansion of his work, Falwell began selling bonds to investors in his ministry. The investment program was not professionally organized or audited, and it triggered an investigation by the Securities and Exchange Commission (SEC). In 1973 the SEC charged Thomas Road with fraud and deceit for misleading investors, and newspapers reported that the church was near insolvency. The SEC recommended that the church and its property go into receivership. Despite a flurry of negative media stories, a federal judge determined that Falwell had not intentionally deceived his investors. Falwell and the judge worked out a plan to bring in outside financial experts to oversee the church's administration and money. Through the process, Falwell learned an important lesson. As much as he loved his country, he had no love for the government of the United States.

Shortly after the SEC wrapped up its investigation of Falwell's ministry, another branch of the federal government set its sights on a prominent southern Christian college. Various federal agencies had worked throughout the late 1960s to enforce the provisions of the Civil Rights Act of 1964, which Falwell had opposed. In 1970 the IRS determined that institutions practicing segregation were by definition not charitable and therefore not tax-exempt. The IRS then sought to apply this ruling to Bob Jones University (BJU), a fundamentalist university in South Carolina that had denied admission to African Americans until 1971 and was still prohibiting interracial dating in 1975. BJU challenged the IRS policy and ultimately lost at the U.S. Supreme Court. That the IRS had the power to use its tax codes to shape Christian university policies provoked a significant backlash. Christian supporters of southern segregation, as well as people who simply believed that the government should not be dictating policies to private religious institutions, prepared for battle. Large numbers of conservatives had long viewed the federal government with suspicion; now they had a specific reason to act (Document 9).

FOCUSING ON THE FAMILY

Along with issues of race and education, religious conservatives in the 1970s fretted about changing conceptions of the family. Many Americans had invested heavily in the hierarchical model of the nuclear family with its breadwinning husband/father and supportive homemaker wife/mother, convinced that strong families provided the foundation for a strong nation that could overcome the cold war communist threat. Conservative Catholics and Protestants believed that the youth movements and rebellions of the 1960s and early 1970s signified declining family values and the nation's move away from its moral foundations. As a result, evangelicals sought to explain clearly what it meant to be a Christian husband and wife (Document 20).

Conservatives felt particularly threatened by the growing feminist movement, which challenged prevailing models of the family. The battle over the Equal Rights Amendment (ERA), which Congress passed in 1972, highlighted their fears. The ERA stated that "Equality of rights under the law shall not be denied or abridged by the United States or any State on account of sex." As innocuous as this statement may seem, conservatives believed that adding such language to the Constitution would undermine what they saw as the fundamental differences between men and women and that it would open the door to a host of alternative lifestyles, including government support for gay and lesbian rights. When Congress sent the amendment to the states for ratification in 1972, conservatives—many of them women—organized a powerful grassroots opposition.

The most successful anti-ERA organizer was Roman Catholic activist Phyllis Schlafly. Deeply involved in conservative politics, she had long worked to build the right wing of the Republican Party. Linking her model of the family with God and country, she organized a powerful national anti-ERA campaign that helped turn the tide against the amendment (Document 21). Building on the momentum of the campaign, she institutionalized her work in a new conservative organization called the Eagle Forum, which served as a powerful advocacy group for conservative issues. Despite the religious differences that separated Catholics

from evangelicals, they worked together on this as well as on a variety
of other political causes.

Many religious conservatives also opposed the Supreme Court's decision to legalize abortion in *Roe v. Wade* (1973), which, like the ERA,
seemed to undermine traditional gender roles and family values. Throughout U.S. history, abortion had been a fairly common but also somewhat
controversial practice. Many religious leaders in the pre-*Roe* era did
not make a clear distinction between terminating a pregnancy and pre-
venting one through other forms of birth control. Ministers who were
anti-birth control were antiabortion; those who believed that contracep-
tion was an appropriate practice often had few qualms about abortion
when the procedure was performed prior to "quickening" (the time
when a woman begins to feel the fetus move). But beginning in the late
nineteenth century and continuing into the twentieth, doctors working
through the American Medical Association (AMA) lobbied state governments to regulate the practice. Essentially, the AMA argued that doctors, not midwifes or pregnant women themselves, should determine
whether a woman could have an abortion. During the 1950s and into the
1960s, however, the AMA reversed course and began to lobby Congress
and the courts to loosen restrictions. They found an important ally in
the burgeoning feminist movement, which believed that women should
be able to determine for themselves whether or when they would repro-
duce. The Court agreed.

Once the Supreme Court issued its decision in *Roe*, Catholics who
accepted the church's anti-birth control stance felt troubled, while Protestants and Jews had mixed responses. Within a few years, the abortion
controversy moved to the center of cultural debate, and Catholics and
evangelicals began working together. They pressured political candidates on the issue and labored to amend the Constitution to invalidate
Roe. The most radical activists practiced civil disobedience in an effort
to prevent abortions (Documents 16, 17).

The *Roe* decision and the SEC investigation of Falwell's ministry
occurred within months of each other. In the mid-1970s Falwell's growing skepticism about the power of the federal government alongside
the increasing influence of the antiabortion movement pushed him to
rethink his understanding of the relationship between ministry and
politics. He had long affirmed the strict separation of church and state.
But like so many of his generation, including civil rights leaders, he
began to question what exactly that meant. "I thought the separation
doctrine," he explained, "existed to keep the church out of politics. I was
wrong." Thomas Jefferson and the founders, he concluded, had crafted

the First Amendment "to keep the government from interfering with the church." Although the meaning of the First Amendment continues to be subject to intense debate, Falwell's responsibilities seemed obvious to him. "It was my duty as a Christian to apply the truths of Scripture to every act of government."[10]

Falwell came to believe that the United States had turned against God and that only if the American people returned the nation to its supposed Christian foundations would the nation be spared from the wrath of the Almighty. "I doubted seriously," he wrote, "that America would survive the judgment of God because of this 'national sin'" of abortion. Furthermore, "the traditional American family was being threatened" by many things ranging from economic decline to physical and emotional abuse to sexual immorality to divorce.[11]

As Falwell revised his political philosophy, he drew on the work of Francis Schaeffer, a long-haired, goatee-sporting, knickers-wearing guru of modern American evangelicalism. Schaeffer attracted thousands of young evangelical students and intellectuals in the 1960s and 1970s to L'Abri in the Swiss Alps to participate in a unique Christian community. He called on evangelicals to engage better with Western culture and to bring the arts, philosophy, and literature—essentially all of life—under the lordship of Christ. He wrote numerous books, including *How Shall We Then Live?* in 1976, produced a documentary film espousing his ideas, and toured college campuses around the United States. His books sold in the millions. He called on Christians to stem the tide of "secular humanism" and to return the United States to its supposed biblical foundations. A strong abortion opponent, Schaeffer worked with medical doctor (and later Reagan administration surgeon general) C. Everett Koop to produce a film entitled *Whatever Happened to the Human Race?* that graphically described and sensationalized the process of terminating a pregnancy. While Schaeffer never achieved the public notoriety of Falwell, he laid the intellectual foundations for evangelical engagement with modern politics (Document 5).

James Dobson was another evangelical whose family values agenda overlapped with Falwell's in the 1970s and beyond. An expert on child development with a doctorate from the University of Southern California, Dobson, like Falwell, grew increasingly concerned with what he perceived to be the breakdown of the family. In 1970 he published *Dare to Discipline*, a Christian alternative to popular child-rearing manuals that sold millions of copies. Not content to simply diagnose the nation's problems with his pen, in 1977 Dobson founded Focus on the Family

(FOF), which became one of the most influential evangelical organizations in the country. Through FOF Dobson examined day-to-day family issues as well as the ways in which politics, public policy, and legislative decisions affected the family. Blending evangelical Christianity and conservative politics, he immediately began to have an important impact on the broader culture.

In the seventies conservative evangelicals faced yet another challenge in the form of the gay rights movement. Since World War II, gays and lesbians had increasingly been defending their rights. Congress mostly ignored them, but local municipalities around the country began to address their concerns. In 1977, to the outrage of local celebrity Anita Bryant, the city of Miami passed an ordinance protecting homosexual rights similar to those passed in many other large cities. A former Miss Oklahoma, Christian singer, and popular spokesperson for Florida orange juice, Bryant started an organization called Save Our Children (which became "Anita Bryant Ministries") to overturn the local ordinance and to build a national campaign against gay rights. Her opposition to homosexuality stemmed in part from some gay sexual practices. Because homosexuals "eat the forbidden fruit of the tree of life" (sperm), she explained, they were an "abomination" in the eyes of God. When pressed, she acknowledged that heterosexual "eating" of the forbidden fruit was equally abominable. Bryant won the support of many evangelicals like Falwell (Documents 18, 19).[12]

BUILDING THE RELIGIOUS RIGHT

With the world seemingly going to hell, evangelicals' apocalyptic expectations surged in the 1970s. The vast majority believed in the imminent rapture of all Christians to heaven, the rise of the Antichrist, and the battle of Armageddon. They offered nonbelievers both a carrot and a stick: Get saved and you can escape the coming tribulation, or ignore God and face the coming judgment. The Vietnam War, the economic recession, the student movements, the "breakdown" of the family, the oil crisis, and the rise of political Islam, among many other things, convinced Christians that the end was truly near. So did the existence of the state of Israel. Believing that Jesus predicted the restoration of Jews to Palestine as a sign of his imminent return, twentieth-century evangelicals became some of Israel's most passionate supporters. A series of books and sermons popularized the evangelical apocalyptic message, none better than Hal Lindsey's *The Late Great Planet Earth*. It was, according to the *New York Times*, the best-selling nonfiction book of the decade (Document 3).

The conviction that the rise of the Antichrist was imminent did not keep Christians from working through the political system for causes they believed in. In fact, over the next few decades Lindsey routinely blended apocalyptic prognostication with right-wing politics. Many evangelicals, including Falwell, clung to the philosophy described by Boston minister Harold Ockenga in 1945: "We labor as though Christ would not come for a millennium. We live as though he were to come to-night." Battling the legions of Satan presented evangelicals with a win-win opportunity. They interpreted their political losses as necessary events that brought them one step closer to Christ's Second Coming, while their political victories indicated their own righteousness and God's blessing. They knew that God's judgment was imminent; he was going to separate the righteous from the unrighteous, the sheep from the goats. As the apocalypse approached, evangelicals wanted to demonstrate that they were on the right side of history.[13]

In many ways, Falwell represented the prototypical evangelical of the era in that he blended apocalyptic fear-mongering with political activism. In the years after the SEC fight and in response to *Roe*, the ERA debate, the Bob Jones case, the growing gay rights campaign, the implementation of sex education in the public school curriculum, and a host of other issues, Falwell began calling for "all-out political involvement by the Christian community." In 1976 he toured the country with seventy Liberty students to perform a musical program entitled *I Love America* in honor of the nation's bicentennial. In each of the 141 cities Falwell visited, he met with local pastors and lay leaders, encouraging them to step up their political activities. At the end of each program, he delivered a succinct sermon that outlined the nation's moral crisis and God's impending judgment. The tour introduced Falwell to politically interested people all over the nation who began to look to him as a leader among conservative Christians. "This musical presentation," Falwell explained, "was the first offensive we launched to mobilize Christians across America for political action against abortion and the other social trends that menaced the nation's future. We were calling America back to God."[14]

Falwell's was not the only offensive. In the 1970s a handful of evangelical leaders—especially younger students and academics—believed that their movement had placed too much emphasis on the wrong things. While Falwell was building alliances with right-wing partisans, evangelical writers and activists who were more politically progressive, including Ronald Sider and Jim Wallis, called on Christians to pay more attention to issues of race, poverty, and economic justice (Document 4). They also called for what they termed an all-encompassing pro-life position that rejected not only abortion, but also the nuclear arms race, the death penalty, and war. A few prominent African American evangelicals, including Chicago minister Clarence Hilliard, called on Christians to take racism more seriously. *Christianity Today*, which took a moderate stance on issues of race and generally did not support the broader civil rights movement, nevertheless opened its pages to contrasting viewpoints including that of Hilliard (Document 10). Although progressive evangelicals never achieved the success or influence of Falwell and his allies, they have served as a constant reminder that to be evangelical is not necessarily to be a political conservative.

While evangelicals in the mid-1970s had begun to focus on a set of key issues, they had not yet linked those issues to the success of a particular political party. When Baptist Sunday school teacher Jimmy Carter campaigned for the presidency in 1976, a *Newsweek* cover story entitled "Born Again!" indicated that the increasingly important evangelical vote was still up for grabs.[15] The Georgia governor was challenging incumbent Gerald Ford, also an evangelical Christian. When reporters on the campaign trail asked Carter about religion, he responded using typical evangelical language, explaining that he had a "personal relationship" with Jesus Christ. To the press, this sounded bizarre. Kenneth Briggs of the *New York Times* recalled that "many reporters reacted to Jimmy Carter's unabashed espousal of 'born again' Christianity with about as much befuddlement as if Mr. Carter had said he had ridden in a flying saucer." But to his supporters, Carter seemed to be exactly what the country needed. After all, as one southern minister famously exclaimed, his initials were even the same as Jesus Christ's.[16]

Both presidential candidates reached out to the increasingly politically engaged evangelical movement, but neither fully embraced conservative Christians' social concerns. The Republican Party, still reeling from the Watergate scandal, which led to President Richard Nixon's 1974 resignation over allegations that he had broken a series of laws to cover up the misdeeds of his staff, struggled to regain voters' trust. Meanwhile, Carter's decision to grant an interview with *Playboy* magazine disappointed many believers. Despite *Playboy's* reputation for publishing highly respected interviews with important figures, some religious conservatives criticized Carter for working with a magazine best known for publishing nude photographs. Furthermore, in the interview he used the slang term *screw* to describe sex, and he admitted that he had "lusted" in his heart for many women. The latter was a reference to the Sermon on the Mount: "But I say unto you, That whosoever looketh on a woman to lust after her hath committed adultery with her already in his heart" (Matthew 5:28). Although the candidate kept his clothes on for *Playboy*'s photographers, the interview did not go over well with many Christians. Nevertheless, Carter earned almost half of evangelicals' ballots and easily defeated Ford. This was the last time the white evangelical electorate split so evenly.

The Carter presidency proved to be a disappointment for many conservative Christians. Federal agencies under Carter's jurisdiction, including the IRS, seemed to be threatening the autonomy of private religious schools, which angered the faithful. Carter's sponsorship of a White House Conference on Families backfired when social conservatives claimed that liberals had rigged the conference, had shaped the agenda to reflect their beliefs, and had refused to let "pro-family" activists speak. The president's support of the ERA and of gay rights and his conviction that abortion should be legal (even though he was personally opposed to the practice) further quenched many evangelicals' enthusiasm for the Georgian.

During this period Falwell continued to rally Americans to his various causes. In 1978 he launched a second national tour entitled "America, You're Too Young to Die!" and in 1979 he and his Liberty students took their *I Love America* musical program to the steps of the nation's capital. They also performed the show in most of the country's state capitals, where Falwell recruited ministers and lay leaders interested in contributing to his religious-patriotic cause. Rallying the faithful, however, was not enough to secure the changes Falwell wanted to see. He believed that he had to do more.

THE MORAL MAJORITY AND THE REAGAN REVOLUTION

In 1979 Falwell and a small group of activists, including conservative Republican politicos Howard Phillips, Paul Weyrich, and Richard Viguerie, met to discuss plans for organizing the growing number of conservative Christian grassroots activists. They wanted to turn evangelicals into a consistent voting bloc that would bolster the power of the conservative wing of the GOP and push the Republican Party as a whole to the right. During a break, Weyrich and Falwell discussed their mutual interests. "Jerry," Weyrich said, "there is in America a moral majority that agrees about the basic issues. But they aren't organized. They don't have a platform. The media ignore them. Somebody's got to get that moral majority together."[17]

Falwell agreed. But before he could get that moral majority together, he had to deal with some of his own religious prejudices. He claimed that he felt uneasy about working with people who did not share his fundamentalist theological views. In his autobiography, Falwell explained that Francis Schaeffer helped him overcome his prejudices and to join together with "cobelligerents" on social and political issues without compromising issues of faith. Since he was already working with Weyrich, a Catholic, he probably was not really that concerned about the issue, but he did have to justify cross-faith alliances. Schaeffer provided him with the language to do it.

In June 1979 Falwell, Weyrich, and Viguerie incorporated the Moral Majority. The initial board of directors boasted prominent ministers including Tim LaHaye, the pastor of a suburban San Diego church (who is best known as the coauthor of the best-selling apocalyptic *Left Behind* novels). "This was war," Falwell remembered. He believed that "to win the war against crime and immorality, to save the American family, to stop the killing of 1.5 million unborn infants every year would take everyone willing to take a stand regardless of his or her race or religion, social class or political party." Falwell told Christians around the nation that they had a threefold mission: to get people saved, to get them baptized, and to get them registered to vote. He believed that if he could get conservative Christians to the polls, they would turn the tide in the nation. Within a couple of years the Moral Majority represented nearly 7 million people who dedicated themselves to pro-life, pro-family, pro-morality, pro-Israel, and pro-strong-national-defense causes (Document 23). While the organization did not represent all evangelical Christians, it did represent a substantial number of those who wanted to make their political voices heard. Furthermore, through church-based voter registration drives, it succeeded in motivating hundreds of thousands of previously apolitical Christians to get to the polls, most often on behalf of the GOP. Meanwhile, a handful of other prominent ministers including Pat Robertson reinforced Falwell's message, encouraging evangelicals to engage in politics (Document 22).[18]

The 1980 presidential campaign seemed to be a godsend to leaders like Falwell. Politicians of both parties increasingly reached out to religious activists, and Carter even invited the nation's leading evangelicals to the White House for a discussion of the issues that concerned them (Document 24). But Carter's actions were too little, too late.

Ronald Reagan, a former actor and divorcee who did not regularly attend church, spoke the language of evangelicalism fluently and believed in many of the issues that conservative Christians cared about. He was a strident anticommunist, he denounced the decline of the family, he praised the "old-time religion," and he criticized the permissiveness of the sixties generation. He questioned the validity of evolutionary theory and supported the teaching of creationism in the public schools. Despite having signed a bill that dramatically expanded abortion rights when he was governor of California, Reagan denounced the practice of abortion in 1980. He also believed that the federal government had been overreaching for decades and that power needed to be returned to states and local communities. Reagan, Falwell concluded, "seemed to represent all the political positions we held dear. . . . So we threw our growing political weight in his direction."[19]

Falwell called the election of Reagan "the greatest day for the cause of conservatism and American morality in my adult life." Journalists and political scientists credited the newly energized conservative religious activists, including Falwell's Moral Majority and numerous smaller, lesser-known organizations, with helping give the president his margin of victory over Carter. This was borne out by an ABC News–Lou Harris survey that concluded that the Moral Majority had played a large part in getting conservatives to the polls and in helping swing the South from Carter's column to Reagan's. Perhaps more important, Falwell helped turn evangelicals into a voting bloc that the GOP could not ignore. In every election since 1980, the Republican Party has crafted platforms specifically designed to appeal to social conservatives, the so-called Religious Right, and as a result it has carried the majority of the white evangelical vote. [20]

Despite the high expectations of Falwell and his followers, the Reagan presidency did not turn out to be everything that the faithful had hoped for. Once the president took office, he went to work on the economy and on issues of national defense. He always treated leaders of the Religious Right with respect, but their agenda was not his. When he had an opportunity to appoint a new member to the Supreme Court, he chose Sandra Day O'Connor, who had a record of supporting abortion rights. Falwell initially balked, provoking Arizona senator and conservative icon Barry Goldwater to quip that Falwell deserved a "boot . . . right in the ass" for trying to co-opt the conservative agenda. The president gave lip service to the Religious Right's concerns, and he publicly supported its efforts to pass a school prayer amendment and an amendment to overturn *Roe*, but he never made these serious priorities. On national defense, however, he found a lot of common ground with evangelicals. They constituted one of the only religious groups in the nation that supported his hawkish cold war policies and nuclear arms buildup. Reagan relished evangelicals' support and their willingness to sanctify actions that troubled most other people of faith (Documents 25, 26).[21]

In 1984 the Moral Majority along with other Religious Right groups again registered millions of new voters for Reagan. During the campaign, any remaining pretense of the Moral Majority's independence or bipartisanship vanished as Falwell began directly associating the entire

President Reagan with Jerry Falwell in the Oval Office, March 15, 1983
Falwell's successful efforts to organize conservative Christians behind the 1980 candidacy of Ronald Reagan earned him the respect of Republican leaders. During Reagan's two terms in office, the president regularly met with Falwell to discuss the issues that had galvanized the Religious Right.

Democratic Party with evil and immorality. In return, the Religious Right became the most influential interest group within the GOP, even if it never spoke for all evangelical Christians.[22]

To reward Falwell for his efforts, Reagan invited him to the inauguration. During the ceremony, the minister stood next to Vice President George H. W. Bush and his family. Falwell was thrilled with what he had accomplished. In just six years, he wrote, the nation "had moved to the right politically and theologically. Conservatives had become the largest voting bloc coalition in the nation." "The 'Religious Right,'" he confidently concluded, "was now formed and in place forever." The war for the soul of America's culture, however, had just begun.[23]

BEYOND THE MORAL MAJORITY

Although the Religious Right may have secured a semipermanent place in mainstream politics, the Moral Majority had not. Falwell had worked hard to earn a seat at the Republican table, but to hold onto that seat evangelicals had to support vice president and party favorite George H. W. Bush for president in 1988. What they did not expect was that a religious broadcaster and evangelical political activist would make his own run for the nomination. Pat Robertson's campaign in the Republican primaries split the Religious Right. Many grassroots activists supported him, while the leaders of the Religious Right were divided between Robertson and Bush (and a few even liked Catholic candidate Jack Kemp). The 1988 campaign undermined the little unity that had previously existed among the men and women who made up the Moral Majority. Soon after, the organization imploded, officially disbanding in 1989.

Conservative activists were not ready to give up. Out of the ashes of Robertson's 1988 defeat came a new political organization, the Christian Coalition. Organized by Robertson and Republican activist Ralph Reed, the Christian Coalition focused less on national campaigns and more on mobilizing Americans at the grassroots level. The coalition worked to win seats on school boards, city councils, and state legislatures, certain that if its members began at the bottom of the political hierarchy, they

Opposite: Jerry Falwell Sliding Down Waterslide, September 10, 1987
In this now iconic image, Jerry Falwell glides down the fifty-two-foot-long waterslide at a Christian theme park. Falwell had vowed to take the plunge in his suit to mark the completion of a successful fundraising campaign.

would slowly begin to have an influence at the national level. Reed promised, "We think the Lord is going to give us this nation back one precinct at a time, one neighborhood at a time, and one state at a time. . . . We're not going to win it all at once with some kind of millennial rush at the White House." During the 1990s Christian Coalition candidates experienced both tremendous victories and heart-wrenching defeats. Their efforts ultimately paid off with the election of professed evangelical and social conservative George W. Bush in 2000. The Religious Right finally helped put a man who shared its values, vision, and agenda in the White House.[24]

Despite Falwell's claim when he left the Moral Majority that he was through with politics, he spent the rest of his career speaking out on many issues. His statements and ideas often sparked controversy, none more so than his reaction to the September 11, 2001, terrorist attacks on the United States. Appearing on Pat Robertson's television show just after the tragedy, Falwell explained that the "sins" of the United States had so angered God that he withdrew his protection from the country. He told Robertson, "I really believe that the pagans, and the abortionists, and the feminists, and the gays and the lesbians who are actively trying to make that an alternative lifestyle, the ACLU, People For the American Way, all of them who have tried to secularize America. I point the finger in their face and say 'you helped this happen.'" He later apologized, but this kind of over-the-top rhetoric made Falwell one of the most controversial leaders in the nation.[25]

In recent years, the founding generation of the Religious Right has slowly faded from the scene. Jerry Falwell died in 2007 (Document 27), James Dobson has retired, and Pat Robertson and Phyllis Schlafly are spending less and less time in the spotlight. Nevertheless, the complicated and contested relationships between religion and politics don't show any signs of ebbing. Republicans continue to masterfully link God and values to their campaigns, while Democrats too have grown far more comfortable talking publicly about religion. Whether this is good for the nation, or for the nation's religious communities, is hotly debated. What is clear is that religion will continue to play an important role in American politics and culture for years, and probably generations, to come. In part, we have Jerry Falwell to thank or to blame for that.

NOTES

[1] Howell Raines, "Reagan Backs Evangelicals in Their Political Activities," *New York Times*, August 23, 1980.

[2] Jerry Falwell, *Falwell: An Autobiography* (Lynchburg, Va.: Liberty House Publishers, 1997), 117.

3Ibid., 118, 125.

4For a smart analysis of Falwell's autobiography, see Susan Friend Harding, *The Book of Jerry Falwell: Fundamentalist Language and Politics* (Princeton, N.J.: Princeton University Press, 2000).

5Ralph T. Davis to W. B. Riley, November 25, 1941, and W. B. Riley to Ralph T. Davis, December 5, 1941, Box 1, Collection 113 (unprocessed), Papers of the National Association of Evangelicals (Wheaton College Archives, Wheaton, Ill.).

6See Steven P. Miller, *Billy Graham and the Rise of the Republican South* (Philadelphia: University of Pennsylvania Press, 2009).

7Falwell, *Falwell*, 224.

8On Falwell's business ventures, see Dirk Smillie, *Falwell Inc.: Inside a Religious, Political, Educational, and Business Empire* (New York: St. Martin's Press, 2008).

9Falwell, *Falwell*, 308, 312; Jerry Falwell, *Ministers and Marches* (Lynchburg, Va.: Thomas Road Baptist Church, 1965).

10Falwell, *Falwell*, 360.

11Ibid., 363, 365.

12"Playboy Interview: Anita Bryant," *Playboy* (May 1978), 78.

13Harold John Ockenga, "Jesus Christ Is Coming from Heaven—So What?" (April 15, 1945), 10, Sermon Manuscripts, Harold John Ockenga Papers (Gordon Conwell Theological Seminary, South Hamilton, Mass.).

14Falwell, *Falwell*, 365, 368.

15Kenneth L. Woodward, John Barnes, and Laurie Lisle, "Born Again," *Newsweek* (October 25, 1976), 68–70, 75–76, 78.

16Kenneth A. Briggs, "An Evangelical's Rise," *New York Times*, July 30, 1977.

17Falwell, *Falwell*, 384.

18Ibid., 389.

19Ibid., 390.

20Kenneth Briggs, "Dispute on Religion Raised by Campaign," *New York Times*, November 9, 1980; John D. Lofton Jr., "Pollster Harris Credits Moral Majority Vote for Reagan's Stunning Landslide Win," *Conservative Digest* (December 1980): 13.

21Michael Tackett, "Barry Goldwater, '64 Nominee, Dies," *Chicago Tribune*, May 30, 1998.

22On the role of evangelicals in the 1980s campaigns, see Daniel K. Williams, *God's Own Party: The Making of the Christian Right* (New York: Oxford University Press, 2010).

23Falwell, *Falwell*, 406, 425.

24"Robertson Regroups 'Invisible Army' into New Coalition," *Christianity Today* (April 23, 1990), 35.

25"Falwell Apologizes to Gays, Feminists, Lesbians," *CNN*, September 14, 2001 (http://articles.cnn.com/2001-09-14/us/Falwell.apology_1_thomas-road-baptist-church-jerry-falwell-feminists?_s=PM:US).

PART TWO

The Documents

1

Modern Evangelicalism Comes of Age

1

HAROLD JOHN OCKENGA

The "New" Evangelicalism

1957

*As pastor of the historic Park Street Church on Boston Common, found-
ing president of both the National Association of Evangelicals and Fuller
Theological Seminary, and chairman of the board of* Christianity Today
*(evangelicals' magazine of record), Harold John Ockenga was among the
most important and influential evangelicals of the twentieth century. This
sermon, delivered in 1957, represents new evangelicals' efforts to distinguish themselves from the negative stereotypes that had characterized
their interwar fundamentalist predecessors as well as those Christians
who in the 1950s still carried the flag of militant, separatist fundamentalism. Eventually many fundamentalist stalwarts like Falwell would adopt
the philosophy of Christian social activism articulated here.*

Social questions are pressing in upon everybody. There is the possibility of sudden destruction which is highlighted by Sputnik and Mutnik.[1]
And the racial tensions which are highlighted by the problem of integration. And the mental problems which are exhibited in delinquency and

---

[1] Sputnik refers to the Soviets' successful launch of the world's first artificial satellite,
which symbolized the start of the U.S.-USSR space race. "Mutnik" was the name Americans gave to the dog that the Soviets launched into space later that year.

Harold John Ockenga, "The New Evangelicalism," in *Park Street Spire* (Boston, 1958),
2–7, Harold John Ockenga Papers, Gordon Conwell Theological Seminary, South Hamilton, Mass.

in the growth of the practice of psychiatry. Then the escapism on the part of people illustrated by alcoholism and resort to narcotics. These social problems are facing men today in every realm.

Now is it enough for us to say in answer to this that there is forgiveness for you in the Gospel, there is a new place in the church of Jesus Christ, there is a life which is to come and it is our duty as a church to take this Gospel and these glad tidings unto the world? Is that enough? Or is it necessary for us to carry this message of Christianity beyond doctrine and beyond experience of personal salvation into an application to the social scene? This is the question. Is not, we might add, the social gospel when taken alone a truncated Christianity? And likewise is not the personal gospel when taken alone also a truncated Christianity? Is there not something more? Well, it is here that the new evangelicalism comes in.

The new evangelicalism declares that it is going to face these societal questions. It will do what fundamentalism was not willing to do. Fundamentalism evaded these questions, but the new evangelicalism declares that it will face these questions — face them with Christianity both as doctrine and ethics (both personal and social). Therefore we approach this problem of the new evangelicalism in this broad background of the historical truth. . . .

In the theological treatises of historical movements, it would be said that the social gospel is modernistic, that it is grounded on a humanitarian Christology. It thinks only of Jesus as a man, and upon the goodness of mankind, and upon the inevitability of progress, and upon the uniting of utopian idealism to the Kingdom of God. All this proved historically in the development of the social gospel about 1870 when business became so big, and social injustice and corruption and misery increased, and men felt that the Gospel of Christ should be applied also to the social scene. So they began talking about a saved man and a saved society, and there were men like Shailer Mathews, Josiah Strong, Washington Gladden, Harry F. Ward, Reinhold Niebuhr and others who have given themselves to what is called "the social gospel," believing that Christianity has its primary application and influence in the societal problems of life.

The Christians who have been evangelical, fundamentalist, orthodox, have had the highest hope that if we would get people converted, if we would get people to know Christ and if we would get their hearts right, this would carry over into every phase of society. But, unfortunately, it isn't true. Unfortunately, we find a great many Christians who have blind spots on matters of social justice, on matters of racial tensions, on matters of social amelioration of misery of men in one form or another, and the carry-over isn't there. It isn't sufficient to say unto a man, "If you get saved, all your mental problems will be solved." It isn't sufficient to say, "If you get saved, you will be well physically." It isn't sufficient to say, "If you get saved, all social problems will be solved." It doesn't happen that way. And, as a result of it, we must have not only a personal presentation of the Christian faith, but there must be the carry-over of this into society itself. And here is where the new evangelicalism comes in.

The new evangelicalism would say concerning the social gospel that it by itself will lead to the welfare state, to creeping socialism and ultimately to Communism. It predisposes men toward Communism. On the other hand, the new evangelical would say this, that the personal Gospel is isolated when it leaves out the social consciousness and may lead individuals to look for pie in the sky and forget all about their relationship to their fellow men. . . .

The new evangelicalism . . . declares that it accepts the authority of the Bible, a plenarily-inspired Bible that is historically trustworthy and authentic. The new evangelical is one who still stands on the Bible. He breaks with the modernist, however, in reference to his embrace of the full orthodox system of doctrine against that which the modernist has accepted. He breaks with the fundamentalist on the fact that he believes that the Biblical teaching, the Bible doctrine and ethics, must apply to the social scene, that there must be an application of this to society as much as there is an application of it to the individual man.

Let us look then for a moment at the deficiencies of fundamentalism. First of all, let me say that fundamentalism is an honorable word. It is embraced by many eminent men whom we hold in highest esteem, and honor and friendship. We believe that fundamentalism is right as far as doctrine is concerned, and we embrace it and, if it were confined to that, I would like to be called a fundamentalist. But we believe that fundamentalism is wrong in its social approach and social philosophy. . . .

Well, then, what is the direction in which the evangelical then should go? First of all, the evangelical embraces creedal Christianity — Christianity as expressed in the confessions of the church which is New Testament Christianity grounded upon the acceptance of the Bible as the Word of God, as plenarily inspired, and authoritative and infallible. Now on the basis of that Bible, all of the doctrines of orthodoxy which I need not mention now are embraced by the new evangelicalism. This is their view. And this has a carry-over into the social scene so that there is an application of this unto the problems of the day so that our view of God, and of man, and of the church, and of society, and of sin, and of salvation must have its effects upon the social problem of the day.

What about the strategy? The new evangelical believes in positive preaching of the Word and of the doctrines of Scripture, as opposed to error, but not delving in personalities. The evangelical believes that the Gospel is the power of God unto salvation, that it will convict, that it will convert, that it will change, and that this Gospel is intellectually defensible and respectable in the face of all of the onslaughts of the day. The evangelical is willing to face the intellectual problems whether they deal with creation, or with the age of man, or whatever it is, examining the claims of the Bible itself concerning inspiration and revelation and to state those in the light of the best knowledge of the day in which it lives. The evangelical is unafraid of this and he believes in the positive, aggressive, constructive presentation of the Word that there can be fruit that is given to it as God has promised that it will come. . . .

Do you see what that means? That means that there has evolved today a different emphasis, a different theological application of orthodox Christianity and one that is dynamic and virile and strong, one that is able to say, "Christ is the answer." "Christ is the answer to your sin problem. Christ is the answer in the Biblical framework of reference because there is no other Christ. Christ is the answer when He and His teachings and Biblical Christianity become translated into the framework of the social picture in which we live."

Beloved, this is the new evangelicalism, and we believe that this evangelicalism not only has a message for each individual and for a student, but that also it will present Biblical Christianity in such a way that it is going to bear a powerful influence upon our society.

2

BILLY GRAHAM

America at the Crossroads

1958

Billy Graham is one of the most significant and media-savvy revivalists in American history. This sermon, originally delivered on the ABC national radio network and then reprinted as a tract, represents his—and many other evangelicals'—efforts to relate faith to country at the height of the cold war as well as to express their concerns about the direction they thought the nation was heading.

As a nation once dedicated to the worship of God and the pursuit of the Christian life, we have lost the respect of the world because we have forsaken these principles on which our nation was founded. We Americans do not realize how unimpressed the rest of the world is by our materialism.

We cannot possibly believe that a person can be happy without a refrigerator or a television set. We cannot possibly believe that there are moral and spiritual principles more important to millions than even a plate of food. We Americans have put the emphasis on the secular and the material so long that we have an idea that the rest of the world must want what we have. I have found in my travels all over the world that they are far more interested in our culture, moral strength and religious heritage than they are in our latest gadgets. . . .

The rest of the world reads about our mad scramble for material things, our occupation with pleasure, and our obsession with sex. They read about our crime rate and racial tensions. I have found that people all over the world are ignorant of the fact that millions of Americans do go to church and do believe in God. They do not think of us as a nation that acts on the basis of moral principle, but rather expediency. They think of our military bases around the world as a plan to save our own skins rather than to protect that which is morally right.

Billy Graham on "The Hour of Decision," from Billy Graham, *America at the Crossroads* (Minneapolis: Billy Graham Evangelistic Association, 1958).

We have given place to the accursed thing of materialism. We have made the mistake of putting prosperity, security and comfort ahead of the spiritual ideals upon which our nation was founded.

In the year 1787 Edward Gibbon wrote, "The Decline and Fall of the Roman Empire." Here was a nation that held a striking parallel to America today. Once the leader in world affairs, her leadership was threatened. She was rich and prosperous with an economy that defied collapse. Her armies were respected by the nations and her sprawling interests covered vast areas of the world. But Rome fell! Proud, vaunted, clever, sophisticated and shrewd Rome fell to a barbarian horde that had far less of material things than Rome had.

These vandals from the north were a dedicated, disciplined, hard, atheistic people. The Romans used to laugh at their ignorance, superstition and lack of military equipment. Mr. Gibbon proved in his book that Rome did not fall because of the military power of the barbarians but rather because of decadence within the Roman culture. He gave five reasons why Rome fell, and I would like to give them to you today because these same five reasons are apparent in American life at this time.

First: The rapid increase of divorce.

A nation never falls until it starts to decay at the center, and the home is the very center of our society. When the dignity and the sanctity of the home, which is the basis of society, is threatened, the whole structure is destined to fall.

Today in this country our morals would put Sodom and Gomorrah to shame. We make jokes about the moral defection of men and women, and we call anyone a prude who raises his voice against our obsession with sex. Our newspapers were filled with a Hollywood love triangle not too long ago. A famous newspaper gossip columnist, laughing about it, said the young man in the triangle was dying; but then the columnist jokingly said, "What a way to die."

This has become our attitude toward the sanctity of the home. It seems that the star that can have the most husbands or wives is the best box office attraction. One of the newest of the sex idols boasts about her number of lovers, and her pictures are attracting larger audiences than the best dramatic films produced. This is a sad commentary on the American people. As a result of our love for the accursed thing, a blight has been put on our homes and children. We now have the highest divorce rate of any nation on earth, and our children are paying the price for their parents' folly.

Secondly: Gibbon said Rome fell because of higher and higher taxes, and the spending of public monies for free bread and circuses for the populace. The average American is now so used to deficit spending that he cannot possibly realize that we are on the broad road that leads to the destruction of our national economy.

Many of our leading economists have warned that it is only a question of time before our deficit financing will be at the end of its rope. In 1958 alone we went in the red by nearly twelve billions of dollars. This means higher and higher taxes. This was one of the basic reasons that our forefathers left the old country. They wanted to escape the high taxes of Europe. The historian Gibbon listed mounting taxes as one of the reasons for Rome's collapse.

Thirdly: Gibbon listed the mad craze for pleasure. When a nation spends four times as much for pleasure as it does for religious and welfare benevolences, it is getting on shaky foundations. Four times as much cash went through the cash registers of our liquor stores in 1957 as went through the hands of our religious and charitable institutions.

Billions of dollars are squandered every year on nonessentials while the church and benevolent organizations often have difficulty meeting their expenses. Our annual tobacco bill exceeds the amount of money we spend on education. We spend as much on travel and cosmetics as we spend for the operation of all of our homes. American women spent an estimated four billion dollars on beauty aids and services in 1957. We Americans have become obsessed with pleasure and entertainment.

Rome on the decline demanded more artificial stimulants and more exciting and brutal sports. On weekends the arenas were jammed with revelling people who found their greatest pleasure in drinking and gluttony and the sadistic thrills of the gladiator contest.

The television screens that are on continually in our homes, the night clubs that are jammed, the Sunday entertainments that are attracting hundreds of thousands every week, rather than a sign of moral health and national normalcy, could be the death cries of a declining civilization.

Fourthly: Gibbon listed the building of gigantic armaments as a contribution to the fall of Rome. As Rome's international influence became less and less, she had to arm more and more. As her enemies increased and her prestige fell to an all-time low, she had to find her security in armed might.

As American prestige around the world has come to a new low, we are spending more and more on armaments. We are frantically building military bases all over the world. We are desperately trying to line up allies in various military alliances to protect us in the event of war. Our very military emphasis makes a lie out of the motto we have on our coins: "In God We Trust."

We no longer trust in God as a nation to spare us, help us and save us as we have trusted in the past. We are now trusting in our B-58s, Hydrogen bombs and missiles. I tell you, this is not enough! I think that all Americans would agree that we must have military power, but to depend on it for our protection alone is a folly that historians of the future will wonder at. . . .

Lastly: Gibbon listed the decay of religion. One Wednesday, President Eisenhower set aside as a day of prayer. His excellent and challenging proclamation went almost unnoticed in the press. Very few churches called a special day of prayer. Only a hand full of people around the country remembered to pray, yet many of our national religious bodies are boasting about our church membership. We are like Voltaire, the agnostic, who tipped his hat when a religious parade went by. "Have you found God?" asked his companion. "Oh, no," said Voltaire, "we salute, but we don't speak."

Too many of us pay our respects to God but we really aren't on speaking terms with Him. We tell our children they ought to pray, but we never go to prayer meeting. Many people take their children to church, then go home to read the Sunday paper. Religion to many of us has lost its vitality, its joy and its urgency.

As in the last days of Rome, religion to the rank and file has faded into mere form, has lost its relevance to life and holds no central allegiance in our lives. When a nation loses its faith, it loses its character; and when it loses its character, it loses its purpose for living; and when it loses its purpose for living, it loses its will to survive.

I am convinced that America stands at the crossroads of her national destiny. One road leads to destruction, and the other leads to prosperity and security. At the moment, we are going down the broad road that leads to destruction. We are going the way of Rome rather than the way of the cross.

Many of you will blame the Republicans or the Democrats. It is not the politicians that should take the blame. It is the American people as individuals. We backslide as individuals before we begin to decay as a nation. Fortunately, there is time to repair the breach. We are still on this side of judgment, though time is quickly passing by. God is sounding the warning. "Today, if you will hear His voice, harden not your heart." "Today is the day of salvation." "The Spirit and the Bride say, Come."

Rome's fate need not be ours if we repent and turn to God.

How shall we escape if we neglect so great a salvation?

Thus today the greatest contribution you can make to your nation is to give your life and your heart to Jesus Christ because when you make your decision for Christ, it is America through you making its decision for Christ and trust in God.

3

HAL LINDSEY

The Late Great Planet Earth

1970

Working with young people in Southern California at the height of the counterculture, Hal Lindsey sought new ways to make the gospel relevant for modern times. One of the results was The Late Great Planet Earth, *the best-selling nonfiction book of the 1970s, with more than 15 million copies sold. It represents the strong apocalyptic strain embedded in most evangelicals' theology. Lindsey believed that the Bible laid out a series of clear signs, such as the restoration of Jews to Palestine, that foreshadowed the rapture of Christians from the earth, the rise of the Antichrist, and the battle of Armageddon. Lindsey used this book to warn the nation of the devastation that was soon to come. Nevertheless, the conviction that the world was about to end did not dissuade Christians like Lindsey, Falwell, and Tim LaHaye from engaging in politics.*

You know, I used to come to the beach to get away from things. Just the relaxing of the waves pounding the shore. But now even the ocean is a reminder that man may be running out of time. Scientists tell us today that we are approaching a time when the ocean may not be able to sustain life anymore.

The Secretary General of the UN recently told us that man has perhaps ten years to solve the problem of survival. He pointed out the three great crises which are unique to this generation—the problem of nuclear weapons, the problem of over-population, the population explosion, the problem of pollution of our air and water. And he said that if we

From Hal Lindsey, *The Late Great Planet Earth* (Grand Rapids, Mich.: Zondervan Publishing House, 1970), 2, 52–58, 135–38, 144, 181–88.

don't solve these problems in this decade, we are approaching the time when they will be beyond our capacity to control. Many are, for this reason, trying to find a way of predicting the future. Computer programs are being set up to try to project which might be the future of man. Many are even turning to astrology and witchcraft.

I believe this generation is overlooking the most authentic voice of all, and that's the voice of the Hebrew prophets. They predicted that as man neared the end of history as we know it that there would be a precise pattern of events which would loom up in history. Nations would fit into a certain power pattern. And all of this would be around the most important sign of all—that is the Jew returning to the land of Israel after thousands of years of being dispersed. The Jew is the most important sign to this generation. . . .

Jesus the Prophet

Jesus Christ also pinpointed the general time of His return when His disciples asked Him two important questions. "What will be the sign of your coming?" they wanted to know. And "What will be the sign of the end of the age?"

The "coming" referred to in the question above is commonly referred to as the second advent of Christ. It was only natural that they wanted to know what signs would indicate His return to set up God's promised Kingdom.

In answer Jesus gave many general signs involving world conditions which he called "birth pangs." He said that these signs, such as religious apostasy,[1] wars, national revolutions, earthquakes, famines, etc., would increase in frequency and intensity just like birth pangs before a child is born.

One of the great signs He predicted, however, is often overlooked. He speaks of the Jewish people being in the land of Palestine as a nation at the time of His return. . . .

Jesus said that this would indicate that He was "at the door," ready to return. Then He said, "Truly I say to you, *this generation* will not pass away until all these things take place" (Matthew 24:34 NASB).

What generation? Obviously, in context, the generation that would see the signs—chief among them the rebirth of Israel. A generation in the Bible is something like forty years. If this is a correct deduction, then within forty years or so of 1948, all these things could take place.

---

[1] The term *apostasy* refers to the abandonment or falling away from the true faith.

Many scholars who have studied Bible prophecy all their lives believe that this is so.

The Repossession of Jerusalem

Another important event that had to take place before the stage would be fully set for the "seven-year countdown" was the repossession of ancient Jerusalem. . . .

There remains but one more event to completely set the stage for Israel's part in the last great act of her historical drama. This is to rebuild the ancient Temple of worship upon its old site. . . .

There is one major problem barring the construction of a third Temple. That obstacle is the second holiest place of the Moslem faith, the Dome of the Rock. This is believed to be built squarely in the middle of the old temple site.

Obstacle or no obstacle, it is certain that the Temple will be rebuilt. Prophecy demands it. . . .

With the Jewish nation reborn in the land of Palestine, ancient Jerusalem once again under total Jewish control for the first time in 2600 years, and talk of rebuilding the great Temple, the most important prophetic sign of Jesus Christ's soon coming is before us. This has now set the stage for the other predicted signs to develop in history. It is like the key piece of a jigsaw puzzle being found and then having the many adjacent pieces rapidly fall into place.

For all those who trust in Jesus Christ, it is a time of electrifying excitement. . . .

One small step for a man — one giant leap for mankind.
   — Apollo 11 Commander Neil Armstrong, 20 July 1969

The Ultimate Trip

And the world caught its breath. Science fiction had prepared man for the incredible feats of the astronauts, but when the reality of the moon landing really hit, it was awesome.

On that historic Sunday in July we watched TV, laughing as Armstrong and Buzz Aldrin loped on the moon's surface. We walked out the front door and looked up at the Old Man and said, "It's really happening—there are a couple of guys walking around up there right now. Amazing."

Astounding as man's trip to the moon is, there is another trip which many men, women, and children will take some day which will leave the rest of the world gasping. Those who remain on earth at that time will use every invention of the human mind to explain the sudden disappearance of millions of people. . . .

RAPTURE—WHAT RAPTURE?

. . . Someday, a day that only God knows, Jesus Christ is coming to take away all those who believe in Him. He is coming to meet all true believers in the air. Without benefit of science, space suits, or interplanetary rockets, there will be those who will be transported into a glorious place more beautiful, more awesome, than we can possibly comprehend. Earth and all its thrills, excitement, and pleasures will be nothing in contrast to this great event.

It will be the living end. The ultimate trip.

If you are shaking your heads over this right now, please remember how many "impossibles" you have said in your lifetime—or how many "impossibles" men throughout the ages have said to many things God has revealed through His spokesmen. And yet they were possible, because nothing is impossible for God.

We have been examining the push of world events which the prophets foretold would lead the way to the seven-year countdown before the return of Jesus Christ to earth. The big question is, will you be here during this seven-year countdown? Will you be here during the time of the Tribulation when the Antichrist and the False Prophet are in charge for a time? Will you be here when the world is plagued by mankind's darkest days?

It may come as a surprise to you, but the decision concerning your presence during this last seven-year period in history is entirely up to you.

God's Word tells us that there will be one generation of believers who will never know death. These believers will be removed from the earth before the Great Tribulation—before that period of the most ghastly pestilence, bloodshed, and starvation the world has ever known. . . .

When will the Rapture occur? We don't know. No one knows. But God knows. However, we believe that according to all the signs, we are in the general time of His coming. . . .

In this chapter I will make a number of forecasts about the future which are based on a careful study of the prophetic truth and the writings of many scholars on the subject. I believe that these forecasts are based upon sound deductions; however, please don't get the idea that I think that I am infallibly right in the same way that a Biblical prophet speaking under the direct inspiration of God's Spirit was. I believe that God today gives us illumination to what has been written, but that He doesn't give us infallible revelation as He gave the authors of the Bible. Here, then, are the things that I believe will happen and develop in the near future. . . .

In the institutional church, composed of professing Christians who are in many cases not Christian, look for many things to happen:

With increasing frequency the leadership of the denominations will be captured by those who completely reject the historic truths of the Bible and deny doctrines which according to Christ Himself are crucial to believe in order to be a Christian. . . .

Secondly, as ministers depart from the truths of the Bible they lose the authority and power that it has to meet real human needs, and as many ministers are not truly born spiritually themselves and are consequently without the illumination of God's Spirit, they no longer will be able to hold their present congregations, much less attract others. So they resort to "social action gimmicks," super-organization, and elaborate programs as a substitute. . . .

Young people will continue to accelerate their exodus from the institutional churches. Several surveys taken by church leaders indicate this. Youth today reject impersonal, highly structured organizations with their emphasis upon buildings and material affluence. In talking with many young people from various backgrounds I have found that the institutional churches are viewed by them as a reflection of all they despise in what they consider materialistic, hypocritical, and prejudiced elements within our American culture.

Above all, young people want a simple, personal, and relevant answer to life that isn't based upon self-centered materialism, but upon real life, selfless love. When they are shown that this idealistic view of life cannot be achieved by various shades of welfarism, socialism, or drugs, but only through a personal relationship with Christ that is not tied to joining an institutional church (or religious country club as they call it), then many respond and receive Jesus Christ. . . .

Many youth are going to be on the front edge of a movement toward first century-type Christianity, with an emphasis upon people and their needs rather than buildings and unwieldy programs. . . .

Keep your eyes on the Middle East. If this is the time that we believe it is, this area will become a constant source of tension for all the world. The fear of another World War will be almost completely centered in the troubles of this area. It will become so severe that only Christ or the Antichrist can solve it. Of course the world will choose the Antichrist.

Israel will become fantastically wealthy and influential in the future. Keep your eyes upon the development of riches in the Dead Sea.

The United States will not hold its present position of leadership in the western world; financially, the future leader will be Western Europe. Internal political chaos caused by student rebellions and Communist subversion will begin to erode the economy of our nation. Lack of moral principle by citizens and leaders will so weaken law and order that a state of anarchy will finally result. The military capability of the United States, though it is at present the most powerful in the world, has already been neutralized because no one has the courage to use it decisively. When the economy collapses so will the military.

The only chance of slowing up this decline in America is a widespread spiritual awakening.

As the United States loses power, Western Europe will be forced to unite and become the standard-bearer of the western world. Look for the emergence of a "United States of Europe" composed of ten inner member nations. The Common Market is laying the groundwork for this political confederacy which will become the mightiest coalition on earth. It will stop the Communist take-over of the world and will for a short while control both Russia and Red China through the personal genius of the Antichrist who will become ruler of the European confederacy.

Look for the papacy to become even more involved in world politics, especially in proposals for bringing world peace and world-wide economic prosperity.

Look for a growing desire around the world for a man who can govern the entire world.

Look for some limited use of modern nuclear weapons somewhere in the world that will so terrify people of the horrors of war that when the Antichrist comes they will immediately respond to his ingenious proposal for bringing world peace and security from war. This limited use could occur between Russia and China, or upon the continental United States. . . .

Look for the present sociological problems such as crime, riots, lack of employment, poverty, illiteracy, mental illness, illegitimacy, etc., to increase as the population explosion begins to multiply geometrically in the late '70's.

Look for the beginning of the widest spread famines in the history of the world.

Look for drug addiction to further permeate the U.S. and other free-world countries. Drug addicts will run for high political offices and win through support of the young adults.

Look for drugs and forms of religion to be merged together. There will be a great general increase of belief in extrasensory phenomena, which will not be related to the true God, but to Satan.

Astrology, witchcraft, and oriental religions will become predominant in the western world.

Where Do We Go from Here?

We believe that in spite of all these things God is going to raise up a believing remnant of true Christians and give one last great offer of the free gift of forgiveness and acceptance in Jesus Christ before snatching them out of the world as it plunges toward judgment. . . .

So let us seek to reach our family, our friends, and our acquaintances with the Gospel with all the strength that He gives us. The time is short.

In the early centuries, the Christians had a word for greeting and departing; it was the word, "maranatha," which means "the Lord is coming soon." We can think of no better way with which to say good-by —

MARANATHA!

4

Chicago Declaration of Evangelical Social Concern
November 25, 1973

In 1973 evangelical scholar Ronald Sider organized a conference of evangelical leaders to discuss the ways in which faith related to social issues. This declaration was the result. The declaration's fifty-three original signatories included women, African Americans, a future congressman, ministers, writers, and scholars. It demonstrated that not all evangelicals agreed with the social conservatism that would come to define the Religious Right just a few years later.

Evangelicals for Social Action, www.evangelicalsforsocialaction.org/document
.doc?id=107.

As evangelical Christians committed to the Lord Jesus Christ and the full authority of the Word of God, we affirm that God lays total claim upon the lives of his people. We cannot, therefore, separate our lives from the situation in which God has placed us in the United States and the world.

We confess that we have not acknowledged the complete claim of God on our lives.

We acknowledge that God requires love. But we have not demonstrated the love of God to those suffering social abuses.

We acknowledge that God requires justice. But we have not proclaimed or demonstrated his justice to an unjust American society. Although the Lord calls us to defend the social and economic rights of the poor and oppressed, we have mostly remained silent. We deplore the historic involvement of the church in America with racism and the conspicuous responsibility of the evangelical community for perpetuating the personal attitudes and institutional structures that have divided the body of Christ along color lines. Further, we have failed to condemn the exploitation of racism at home and abroad by our economic system.

We affirm that God abounds in mercy and that he forgives all who repent and turn from their sins. So we call our fellow evangelical Christians to demonstrate repentance in a Christian discipleship that confronts the social and political injustice of our nation.

We must attack the materialism of our culture and the maldistribution of the nation's wealth and services. We recognize that as a nation we play a crucial role in the imbalance and injustice of international trade and development. Before God and a billion hungry neighbors, we must rethink our values regarding our present standard of living and promote a more just acquisition and distribution of the world's resources.

We acknowledge our Christian responsibilities of citizenship. Therefore, we must challenge the misplaced trust of the nation in economic and military might—a proud trust that promotes a national pathology of war and violence which victimizes our neighbors at home and abroad. We must resist the temptation to make the nation and its institutions objects of near-religious loyalty.

We acknowledge that we have encouraged men to prideful domination and women to irresponsible passivity. So we call both men and women to mutual submission and active discipleship.

We proclaim no new gospel, but the Gospel of our Lord Jesus Christ who, through the power of the Holy Spirit, frees people from sin so that they might praise God through works of righteousness.

By this declaration, we endorse no political ideology or party, but call our nation's leaders and people to that righteousness which exalts a nation.

We make this declaration in the biblical hope that Christ is coming to consummate the Kingdom and we accept his claim on our total discipleship until he comes.

Original Signers:

John F. Alexander
Joseph Bayly
Ruth L. Bentley
William Bentley
Dale Brown
James C. Cross
Donald Dayton
Roger Dewey
James Dunn
Daniel Ebersole
Samuel Escobar
Warren C. Falcon
Frank Gaebelein
Sharon Gallagher
Theodore E. Gannon
Art Gish
Vernon Grounds
Nancy Hardesty
Carl F. H. Henry
Paul Henry
Clarence Hilliard
Walden Howard
Rufus Jones
Robert Tad Lehe
William Leslie
C. T. McIntire
Wes Michaelson

David O. Moberg
Stephen Mott
Richard Mouw
David Nelson
F. Burton Nelson
William Pannell
John Perkins
William Petersen
Richard Pierard
Wyn Wright Potter
Ron Potter
Bernard Ramm
Paul Rees
Boyd Reese
Joe Roos
James Robert Ross
Eunice Schatz
Ronald J. Sider
Donna Simons
Lewis Smedes
Foy Valentine
Marlin Van Elderen
Jim Wallis
Robert Webber
Merold Westphal
John Howard Yoder

5

FRANCIS SCHAEFFER

A Christian Manifesto

1981

Francis Schaeffer, a long-haired, goatee-sporting, knickers-wearing guru of modern American evangelicalism, called on Christians to engage better with Western culture and to bring the arts, philosophy, and literature—essentially all of life—under the lordship of Christ. In the 1970s he grew increasingly interested in political activism, and his ideas helped inspire Falwell to enter politics. This "manifesto" sums up the philosophy that undergirded his life work.

The basic problem of the Christians in this country in the last eighty years or so, in regard to society and in regard to government, is that they have seen things in bits and pieces instead of totals.

They have very gradually become disturbed over permissiveness, pornography, the public schools, the breakdown of the family, and finally abortion. But they have not seen this as a totality—each thing being a part, a symptom, of a much larger problem. They have failed to see that all of this has come about due to a shift in world view—that is, through a fundamental change in the overall way people think and view the world and life as a whole. This shift has been *away from* a world view that was at least vaguely Christian in people's memory (even if they were not individually Christian) *toward* something completely different—toward a world view based upon the idea that the final reality is impersonal matter or energy shaped into its present form by impersonal chance. They have not seen that this world view has taken the place of the one that had previously dominated Northern European culture, including the United States, which was at least Christian in memory, even if the individuals were not individually Christian.

From Francis Schaeffer, *A Christian Manifesto* (Westchester, Ill.: Crossway Books, 1981), 17–24, 131–33.

These two world views stand as totals in complete antithesis to each other in content and also in their natural results—including sociological and governmental results, and specifically including law.

It is not that these two world views are different only in how they understand the nature of reality and existence. They also inevitably produce totally different results. The operative word here is *inevitably*. It is not just that they happen to bring forth different results, but it is absolutely *inevitable* that they will bring forth different results.

Why have the Christians been so slow to understand this? There are various reasons but the central one is a defective view of Christianity. This has its roots in the Pietist movement under the leadership of P. J. Spener in the seventeenth century. Pietism began as a healthy protest against formalism and a too abstract Christianity. But it had a deficient, "platonic" spirituality. It was platonic in the sense that Pietism made a sharp division between the "spiritual" and the "material" world—giving little, or no, importance to the "material" world. The totality of human existence was not afforded a proper place. In particular it neglected the intellectual dimension of Christianity. . . .

True spirituality covers all of reality. There are things the Bible tells us as absolutes which are sinful—which do not conform to the character of God. But aside from these the Lordship of Christ covers *all* of life and *all* of life equally. It is not only that true spirituality covers all of life, but it covers all parts of the spectrum of life equally. In this sense there is nothing concerning reality that is not spiritual.

Related to this, it seems to me, is the fact that many Christians do not mean what I mean when I say Christianity is true, or Truth. They are Christians and they believe in, let us say, the truth of creation, the truth of the virgin birth, the truth of Christ's miracles, Christ's substitutionary death, and His coming again. But they stop there with these and other individual truths.

When I say Christianity is true I mean it is true to total reality—the total of what is, beginning with the central reality, the objective existence of the personal-infinite God. Christianity is not just a series of truths but *Truth*—Truth about all of reality. And the holding to that Truth intellectually—and then in some poor way living upon that Truth, the Truth of what is—brings forth not only certain personal results, but also governmental and legal results.

Now let's go over to the other side—to those who hold the materialistic final reality concept. They saw the complete and total difference between the two positions more quickly than Christians. . . .

They understood not only that there were two totally different concepts but that they would bring forth two totally different conclusions, both for individuals and for society. What we must understand is that the two world views really do bring forth with inevitable certainty not only personal differences, but also total differences in regard to society, government, and law.

There is no way to mix these two total world views. They are separate entities that cannot be synthesized. . . .

The humanist world view includes many thousands of adherents and today controls the consensus in society, much of the media, much of what is taught in our schools, and much of the arbitrary law being produced by the various departments of government.

The term humanism used in this wider, more prevalent way means Man beginning from himself, with no knowledge except what he himself can discover and no standards outside of himself. In this view Man is the measure of all things, as the Enlightenment expressed it. . . .

What does all this mean in practice to us today? I must say, I really am not sure all that it means to us in practice at this moment. To begin, however, it certainly means this: We have been utterly foolish in our concentration on bits and pieces, and in our complete failure to face the total world view that is rooted in a false view of reality. And we have not understood that this view of reality inevitably brings forth totally different and wrong and inhuman results in all of life. This is nowhere more certain than in law and government — *where law and government are used by this false view of reality as a tool to force this false view and its results on everyone.*

It is time we consciously realize that when *any office* commands what is contrary to God's Law it abrogates its authority. And our loyalty to the God who gave this law then requires that we make the appropriate response in that situation to such a tyrannical usurping of power. . . .

We must try to roll back the results of the total world view which considers material-energy, shaped by chance, as the final reality. . . .

As we think about these things, we must think about one other factor: Those who have the responsibility as Christians, as they live under Scripture, must not only take the necessary legal and political stands, but must practice all the possible Christian alternatives simultaneously with taking stands politically and legally.

2

Race and Religious Activism

6

L. NELSON BELL

A Southern Evangelical on Integration

August 17, 1955

A former missionary and medical doctor, L. Nelson Bell became a leading evangelical in the mid-twentieth century and helped found Christianity Today. *His daughter Ruth married Billy Graham, and he served as one of Graham's closest allies and defenders. Bell wrote this article in response to the emerging civil rights movement and, more specifically, to the 1954* Brown v. Board of Education *Supreme Court decision, which struck down segregation in public schools.*

With that temerity often attributed to morons and their like, we would make a few suggestions which might *possibly* help to clarify our thinking on the matter of true Christian race relations.

We are fully aware that what we write will not please extremists on either side of this controversial matter. However, here goes:

Within the scope of those rights prescribed by law, every American citizen is equal. For that reason it is futile to defend any law which restricts the legal rights of any individual, or group of individuals.

Therefore, segregation by law cannot be legally defended. This in no way precludes the expediency, wisdom and right of voluntary

L. Nelson Bell, "Christian Race Relations Must Be Natural—Not Forced." Reprinted from *Southern Presbyterian Journal*, August 17, 1955, 3–5.

alignments along racial or other social lines (and it should not be forgotten for one minute that it is the Christian thing at times to be expedient).

In like manner, *forced integration* cannot be defended, either on legal or moral grounds.

Both forced segregation and forced integration infringe on the legal right of the individual.

The great difficulty in the South today is that too many people are talking at odds because they are talking about different things. Another difficulty stems from those Northern friends who affirm a certain procedure as the only "Christian" procedure and who fail to be realistic even in their own back yards.

At present the discussions in our church are based on three different factors:

A. The decision of the United States Supreme Court, declaring segregation in the public schools to be illegal.

B. The actions of our General Assembly[1] stating that the Christian answer to the race problem is integration of the races within the area of Church relationships.

C. The feeling of many that integration of the races is both impracticable and unwise.

Regardless of the actions outlined in "A" and "B" above, there is a great host of people, represented in "C," who do not have the remotest idea of complying with these actions. Some do this with minds which are prejudiced and utterly un-Christian in their attitudes to the Negro. Some do this from genuine fear, the fear of a minority living in the midst of a majority of another race—this situation is particularly true in certain areas of the deep South. There are others—and they are as Christian in their thinking and practices as any in this world—who believe that it is un-Christian, unrealistic and utterly foolish to *force* those barriers of race which have been established by God and which when destroyed by man are destroyed to his own loss.

There is no possible excuse for the attitude of those who hate people of any race, whether it be Yellow, Black, White or Red. That such hate exists is but a tragic reminder of the sinfulness of the human heart. There is but one Christian attitude between people, regardless of race, and that is that we are *all* equally precious in God's sight and equally in need of His redeeming grace in Christ Jesus. . . .

---

[1] Refers to the Presbyterian Church in the United States (more commonly known as the Southern Presbyterian Church).

It is utterly foolish to think that wishful thinking, an act of the Supreme Court or an act of the General Assembly — any of these — can destroy race distinctions which are God ordained.

In too much of the discussions and actions today there is an attempt to create an *unnatural situation*, to force something, in the name of Christianity, which has nothing whatsoever to do with Christianity.

In communities where there are but few of one race it could be the wise and natural thing to absorb all races into one Church group. But, it is unnatural and forced to bring about integration where separation is desired and desirable. . . .

Our dilemma is caused by those who would force an *unnatural* association, in the name of Christianity. The problem cannot be solved by force, either pro or con. It *must* be solved on the basis of local conditions, and in the light of what would be the *natural* contacts and alignments. This is already done within the confines of each race. The Church has never attempted to force social relationships of any kind. It is an inherent right of the individual to choose his or her own intimate friends and associates and this does not imply anything derogatory to those not so chosen. When that barrier is broken, either within or outside racial lines, the right of the individual is violated. *It is the feeling that just such violation is contemplated by some which makes others both fearful and resentful.*

In this connection we feel constrained to say that the greatest enemies of a solution of the problem are those integrationists who say the ultimate solution of the race issue lies in intermarriage of the races. Not only is this being said but, in some instances, it is being advocated.

With all the restraint we can muster we would ask this question: what possible "solution" is there to be found in crossing racial barriers, barriers which man had no part in making? Such thinking comes from a basic philosophy so distorted and so out of keeping with Christian realism and God-given common sense that it should make all Christians stop and ask for time for prayer and study.

Until the attempts to *force an unnatural situation* are stopped there will be no right solution. . . . There is nothing Christian or natural in *manufacturing* situations for forced relationships whether those relationships be with people of the same race, or some other race.

Too little has been said about where Christian race relations must really begin. They begin in those daily contacts where courtesies, considerations and love should be shown to *everyone*, regardless of color. They begin in divesting our minds and hearts of prejudice and pride and hatred and in treating every other person as we would have them treat us. They begin in looking on every individual who is out of Christ as a person for whom Christ died and who is loved by Him. If this involves membership in the same church as its natural outgrowth, then proceed as a Christian should. But, there is nothing un-Christian in natural selections and preferences and those who would, in the name of Christianity, force other alignments do little credit to the cause they would promote.

7

CARL McINTIRE

A Minister Denounces the Civil Rights Act

March 26, 1964

Always fiery and argumentative, minister Carl McIntire spoke out on most of the major issues of the twentieth century. His letter to President Lyndon Johnson reflects the concerns of many conservative evangelicals as the president sought to push the Civil Rights Act of 1964 through Congress. This letter was published in numerous Christian periodicals.

The President
The White House, Washington, D.C.   March 26, 1964

Dear Mr. President:

Your appeal to the leaders and the pastors of the Southern Baptist churches to work for your Civil Rights legislation is, of course, of great concern to every preacher in the country. Since you told us all at your inauguration that you could not bear this burden alone, you have indeed been the object of special prayer in hundreds of the pulpits of this nation. We want God to keep you and to guide you and to comfort you. . . .

The Civil Rights Bill which is before the Congress has in it elements which are in direct contradiction to the clear and unmistakable teaching of the Bible.

From Carl McIntire to Lyndon Baines Johnson, March 26, 1964, Carl McIntire Papers, Princeton Theological Seminary.

Our Saviour said, "Thou shalt love the Lord thy God with all thy heart, and with all thy soul, and with all thy strength, and with all thy mind; and thy neighbour as thyself." Love is something which is in the heart of man and expresses itself in his deeds and words. The Civil Rights legislation which you are asking the nation to accept is not producing love. In fact, it cannot generate love. And the tensions and conflicts which have developed over this, Mr. President, have actually created bitterness and hate. We are to preach the love of our fellow men and I do not see how we can give you the support which you ask when what you are asking does not produce what Jesus Christ said that we should have.

There are church leaders who have been backing your legislation. But the theological and religious basis on which they ask the people to accept the legislation is not found in holy Scripture. . . . This idea that everybody is a child of God and that the universal brotherhood of man is taught in the holy Scriptures is completely wrong, and yet this legislation is built upon this erroneous concept of man. Those of us who are preachers, and there are thousands of them in the Southern Baptist Church who are preaching every Lord's Day, "Ye must be born again." This doctrine does not support a Civil Rights proposition which is built upon the assumption that all are brothers and it is not necessary to have a new birth.

In another instance, the legislation has embraced an entirely new and different concept as to the use and the responsibility of private property than that which we have found in the Bible and which has been summarized in the great confessions of our various churches in relationship to the Ten Commandments. A man is responsible to God for his property, its use and its disposition. The entire private sector of our society with the individual capitalist and private owner is now to be subject to federal regulation and intervention which gives to the Government a responsibility in this field over private property. At this point we are being told that human rights, therefore, are better and greater than private rights and property rights, and to enforce these so-called superior human rights the federal government takes authority. Those of us who are preachers must preach the moral law as it is set forth in the Ten Commandments and seek to protect the individual in his property from encroachment and attack and destruction by the federal authorities. Your legislation with its present requirements and its broad implications leaves many of us no choice but to oppose it in the name of the righteous law of God.

Further, as preachers we are interested in liberty. God is the Author of liberty and our Saviour said, "If the Son shall make you free, ye shall be free indeed." We are very sensitive to increasing federal direction and control over the lives of all our people. We want nothing to interfere with the free exercise of religion, our freedom of speech, and then the reserved rights under the Constitution to us as individuals, and also to us as States, are a part of the ingredients of liberty. Must the church help that which is going to restrict the liberty of all our people? Have we reached a day when in order to have liberty for the Negro we must restrict the liberty of all? Has it come to a time when in order to preserve liberty we must limit liberty? It appears to many of us that what you are asking us to do is to accomplish by law and police force and federal authority that which can only actually be accomplished by the grace of God and the love which God wants us to have for each other.

Now may I speak very frankly, a spirit of lawlessness and even riot has been stimulated in this country in order to obtain the Civil Rights legislation, and we have waited in vain for any word from your lips as the chief executive which would discourage and denounce such a fundamental assault upon civil order itself. Civil disobedience and some of the disgraceful mob rioting which has been stimulated over this question we feel, Mr. President, should have merited your stern repudiation. When lawlessness and mob action are used to induce legislation and intimidate legislators, the integrity of this Republic is under assault. . . .

It is my firm belief that what this nation needs is not federal legislation such as you are asking, but our people need to be brought face to face with the demands of the eternal law of God as set forth in your mother's Bible. . . .

May I say one final word? When men turn away from the Bible and its teaching, they look to the State and its power. "The Lord is my shepherd; I shall not want" is the opening of the beloved Twenty-third Psalm, the most beloved passage of all the Scripture, and we want the freedom in this land to be able to continue to say that. Instead, it is the federal government is my shepherd; I shall not want. But it is the God of holy Scripture, the God of our fathers, who has brought us this far and blessed us. Why, may I ask, is it that you have not lifted your voice in behalf of the return of the Bible to the public schools, and the return of the use of the name of God and prayer to our public schools? The greatest crisis facing this Republic is our rejection of God. Mr. President, can you not tell the nation that you think our school children ought to have the privilege to pray to Almighty God, and that they should have the privilege of hearing the Ten Commandments read in the public schools of this nation again? You have remained silent on this great question, and this as far as we preachers are concerned is at the heart of the whole question of

Civil Rights and equality and non-discrimination between our peoples, which must be born of mutual respect and love which I say your legislation cannot produce. I have written you directly for I have felt that your appeal calls for it and I assure you that we continue to hold you daily before the Throne of Grace. May our righteous God keep you, guide you, comfort you.

Sincerely,
Carl McIntire

8

JERRY FALWELL

Ministers and Marches

1965

In the midst of the civil rights movement, Jerry Falwell laid out his views on the relationship between church leadership and political activism in this now-famous sermon. He later repudiated the ideas espoused here.

(This message was delivered by Jerry Falwell, pastor of Thomas Road Baptist Church, Lynchburg, Virginia, on Sunday night, March 21, 1965. About 1,000 persons packed the sanctuary to hear this message. Hundreds of others who could not attend asked that this message be put in printed form. Therefore, we humbly make this booklet available.)

Under the Constitution of the United States, every American has the right to "peacefully" petition the government for a redress of grievances. This simply means that, in the present racial crises, all Americans, white, negro, or otherwise, have the legal right to "peacefully" demonstrate in order to obtain voting rights in Alabama—or elsewhere—if these rights are not allowed to the citizens. The purpose of this message is not to question such constitutional rights. Neither is it the intention

From Jerry Falwell, *Ministers and Marches* (Lynchburg, Va.: Thomas Road Baptist Church, 1965), i, 1–4, 6–10, 12–14, 16–17.

of this message to discuss the subject of integration or segregation. It is my desire, in this sermon, to open the Bible and, from God's Word, answer the question— *"Does the 'CHURCH' have any command from God to involve itself in marches, demonstrations, or any other actions, such as many ministers and church leaders are so doing today in the name of civil rights reforms?"*

At the outset of this message, I do wish to speak frankly about one particular matter. There are, no doubt, many very sincere Christians who have felt a compulsion to join in civil rights efforts across the nation. At the same time, I must personally say that I do question the sincerity and non-violent intentions of some civil rights leaders such as Dr. Martin Luther King Jr., Mr. James Farmer, and others, who are known to have left-wing associations. It is very obvious that the Communists, as they do in all parts of the world, are taking advantage of a tense situation in our land, and are exploiting every incident to bring about violence and bloodshed. But I must repeat that I do believe many sincere persons are participating. I must also say that I believe these demonstrations and marches have done more to damage race relations and to gender hate than to help! . . .

Since all orthodox Christians accept the Bible to be the verbally inspired Word of God, let us look into this Bible and see what the commands to the church are. . . .

Nowhere are we commissioned to reform the externals. We are not told to wage wars against bootleggers, liquor stores, gamblers, murderers, prostitutes, racketeers, prejudiced persons or institutions, or any other existing evil as such. Our ministry is not reformation but transformation. The gospel does not clean up the outside but rather regenerates the inside. I have had no greater joy as a minister of the gospel than to witness the marvelous changes wrought in the lives of many people to whom I have preached the gospel. Right here in the Thomas Road Baptist Church, I look into the faces of many people each Sunday who once were involved in the worst kinds of sin. Today they are God-fearing servants of Christ Jesus. What changed them? Did we lead a march down to their bootlegging joint and demand that they stop selling liquor? Did we go to Richmond and try to get laws passed which would send these persons to jail? No! In Christian love, we went to them prayerfully with the message of a crucified Christ. They received this Christ as their own personal Lord and Saviour. When Christ came in, sin went out. They no longer live their former lives. Not because we demanded they stop these things, but because now, they no longer want to do these things. As Paul says it in II Cor. 5:17: "Therefore if any man be in Christ, he is a new creature: old things are passed away; behold, all things are become new." . . .

Phillipians 3:20 is a key verse in getting to the heart of this matter. Paul said "For our citizenship is in Heaven." . . .

We pay our taxes, cast our votes as a responsibility of citizenship, obey the laws of the land, and other things demanded of us by the society in which we live. But, at the same time, we are cognizant that our only purpose on this earth is to know Christ and to make Him known. Believing the Bible as I do, I would find it impossible to stop preaching the pure saving gospel of Jesus Christ, and begin doing anything else — including fighting communism, or participating in civil rights reforms. As a God-called preacher, I find that there is no time left after I give the proper time and attention to winning people to Christ. Preachers are not called to be politicians but to be soul winners. . . .

If the many thousands of churches and pastors of America would suddenly begin preaching the old fashioned gospel of Jesus Christ and the power that is in His atoning blood, a revival would grip our land such as we have never known before. If as much effort could be put into winning people to Jesus Christ across the land as is being exerted in the present civil rights movement, America would be turned upside down for God. Hate and prejudice would certainly be in a great measure overcome. Churches would be filled with sincere souls seeking God. Good relations between the races would soon be evidenced. God is Love, and when He is put first in the individual life and in the church, God's people become messengers of love. May we pray toward this goal.

Jesus Christ and Politics

. . . John 4:6–13 gives the story of Jesus and His meeting with the immoral woman at Jacob's well. Jesus was tired after his long journey into Samaria. A woman of Samaria came to draw water and Jesus asked her for a drink. She replied: "How is it that thou, being a Jew, askest drink of me, which am a woman of Samaria? for the Jews have no dealings with the Samarians." This woman was saying to Jesus that the Jews were segregated from the Samaritans. They discriminated against the Samaritans. It was much like many of the situations existing today in America and in other countries between different nations and races. But as we read the rest of the account, we see that Jesus totally ignored her attempt to involve Him in a discussion about segregation. He immediately began to tell her that her need was spiritual water. He told her all about her sinful life and her great need of salvation. She was converted and then, through her testimony, her home town turned to God. Jesus could have spent the rest of the day telling her how terrible it was for her to be a segregationist. He did not. He told her that her need was in the heart. She was a prejudiced person because she was a sinner in need of a Saviour. He did not work from the outside in, but rather from the inside out. . . .

In relation then to this subject under discussion, I would ask a question: "Does this present civil rights program promote the Love of God?" The leaders are always crying out against prejudice and hate. They are always talking about love. Romans 12:9 says "Let love be without hypocrisy." I am fearful that all of the rioting and demonstrating has produced a great amount of hate as evidenced through the recent murders and other forms of violence. . . .

While the church leaders are so obsessed with the alleged discrimination against negroes in the South, very little is said about the same situation in the North. Likewise, very little is said about the very bad conditions under which American Indians live today. This leads one to believe that political expedience is somewhat involved in this so-called freedom movement. Could it possibly be that the American Indians do not present the potential of a strong voting block in the future? One cannot help but wonder. . . .

As Christians, we detest discrimination. But we do need to see that we can never stop it through any other means than that weapon which was given the church 2,000 years ago—the preaching of the gospel of Christ. . . .

Love cannot be legislated. Love is found in a Person—His Name is Jesus Christ. The church needs to become dedicated once again to the task of preaching Christ. Education, medicine, social reform, and all the other external ministries cannot meet the needs of the human soul and spirit. If money and education could raise the moral standards of a nation, America would be pure indeed. It cannot be done this way. When the light of the gospel shines into the sinner's heart, his entire life and attitudes are transformed.

I feel that we need to get off the streets and back into the pulpits and into the prayer rooms. I believe we need to take our Bibles and go down into the highways and hedges and bring men to Christ. I believe we need to rededicate ourselves to the great task of turning this world back to God. The preaching of the gospel is the only means by which this can be done.

9

Bob Jones University v. United States
1981, 1983

---

*In 1970 the Internal Revenue Service revoked the tax-exempt status of
Bob Jones University (BJU) and other private schools that practiced
racial discrimination. The university fought the IRS in a series of court
battles for more than a decade. The BJU suit eventually made its way to
the U.S. Supreme Court, which ruled in favor of the IRS. That the federal
government, through its tax policies, could indirectly affect policy in private Christian schools troubled many conservative evangelicals, especially
in the South. The first document, an amicus curiae (friend of the court)
brief was submitted by the National Association of Evangelicals with the
goal of persuading the justices to rule in BJU's favor. The second document is Chief Justice Warren Burger's opinion.*

Brief of National Association of Evangelicals As Amicus Curiae in Support of Petitioner

Evangelicals can and do differ with one another in the interpretation
of Scripture. (Most evangelicals would not agree with the view of Bob
Jones University that interracial dating and marriage is contrary to
Scripture.) But they are united in their affirmation of the truth and inspiration of the Bible, as well as the Lordship and Deity of Jesus Christ.

The ominous threat to religious freedom posed by the decision of the
court below compels us to submit this brief....

Bob Jones University believes that the Bible forbids interracial marriage. In order to enforce this religious view, the University barred
admission of black students prior to September, 1971. After that date
married black students were admitted, and since May, 1975, a completely
open admissions policy has been in effect. The earlier policy excluding
all or most blacks was followed as the easiest and most reliable way to

---

The National Association of Evangelicals Amicus Curiae Brief re: *Bob Jones University
v. The United States* (1981); and Chief Justice Warren Burger's opinion re: *Bob Jones
University v. The United States* (1983). Available on LexisNexis.

protect its religious conviction against interracial dating and marriage. Restrictions designed to enforce this view continue to exist; discipline is applied with an even hand.

The court below has ignored crucial factual differences in the cases it relies upon, such as the total exclusion of blacks from educational institutions. In so doing, it erroneously applies a public policy intended to rid this nation of invidious racial discrimination to a University which admits blacks, but follows a policy with respect to interracial dating and marriage based not on personal bias or prejudice, but sincere religious belief.

NAE is familiar with the University and its strict theological views, including its religiously based nonmiscegenation belief. We would not submit this brief on behalf of the University if we had reason to believe that its professed religious beliefs were being used to mask invidious racial discrimination. . . .

We are also deeply disturbed at the precedential potential of the lower court's decision with respect to the Government's use of other clearly defined public policies, such as the policy against sex discrimination, as the basis for withdrawing tax exemption. What the Government might view as a violation of the public policy against sex discrimination, evangelicals would consider faithful adherence to Scriptual teaching with respect to the proper roles of women within the church. For example, many evangelical churches do not believe in the ordination of women as pastors or elders. Left intact, the decision of the court below will inevitably be used to justify subordination of religious belief to current notions of public policy, and the compass of § 501(c)(3) of the Internal Revenue Code will be merely a function of an ever changing public policy continuum.

Bob Jones University v. United States

Chief Justice Burger delivered the opinion of the Court.

We granted certiorari to decide whether petitioners, nonprofit private schools that prescribe and enforce racially discriminatory admissions standards on the basis of religious doctrine, qualify as tax-exempt organizations. . . .

Until 1970, the Internal Revenue Service granted tax-exempt status to private schools, without regard to their racial admissions policies, under § 501(c)(3) of the Internal Revenue Code, 26 U. S. C. § 501(c)(3), and granted charitable deductions for contributions to such schools. . . .

On January 12, 1970, a three-judge District Court for the District of Columbia issued a preliminary injunction prohibiting the IRS from according tax-exempt status to private schools in Mississippi that discriminated as to admissions on the basis of race. . . .

Bob Jones University is a nonprofit corporation located in Greenville, S.C. Its purpose is "to conduct an institution of learning . . . , giving special emphasis to the Christian religion and the ethics revealed in the Holy Scriptures.". . . The corporation operates a school with an enrollment of approximately 5,000 students, from kindergarten through college and graduate school. Bob Jones University is not affiliated with any religious denomination, but is dedicated to the teaching and propagation of its fundamentalist Christian religious beliefs. It is both a religious and educational institution. Its teachers are required to be devout Christians, and all courses at the University are taught according to the Bible. Entering students are screened as to their religious beliefs, and their public and private conduct is strictly regulated by standards promulgated by University authorities.

The sponsors of the University genuinely believe that the Bible forbids interracial dating and marriage. To effectuate these views, Negroes were completely excluded until 1971. From 1971 to May 1975, the University accepted no applications from unmarried Negroes, but did accept applications from Negroes married within their race.

Following the decision of the United States Court of Appeals for the Fourth Circuit . . . prohibiting racial exclusion from private schools, the University revised its policy. Since May 29, 1975, the University has permitted unmarried Negroes to enroll; but a disciplinary rule prohibits interracial dating and marriage. That rule reads:

"There is to be no interracial dating.

"1. Students who are partners in an interracial marriage will be expelled.

"2. Students who are members of or affiliated with any group or organization which holds as one of its goals or advocates interracial marriage will be expelled.

"3. Students who date outside of their own race will be expelled.

"4. Students who espouse, promote, or encourage others to violate the University's dating rules and regulations will be expelled."

The University continues to deny admission to applicants engaged in an interracial marriage or known to advocate interracial marriage or dating.

Until 1970, the IRS extended tax-exempt status to Bob Jones University. . . . On January 19, 1976, the IRS officially revoked the University's tax-exempt status, effective as of December 1, 1970, the day after the University was formally notified of the change in IRS policy. . . .

Few social or political issues in our history have been more vigorously debated and more extensively ventilated than the issue of racial discrimination, particularly in education. Given the stress and anguish of the history of efforts to escape from the shackles of the "separate but equal" doctrine of *Plessy v. Ferguson*, 163 U.S. 537 (1896), it cannot be said that educational institutions that, for whatever reasons, practice racial discrimination, are institutions exercising "beneficial and stabilizing influences in community life" . . . or should be encouraged by having all taxpayers share in their support by way of special tax status.

There can thus be no question that the interpretation of § 170 and § 501(c)(3) announced by the IRS in 1970 was correct. That it may be seen as belated does not undermine its soundness. It would be wholly incompatible with the concepts underlying tax exemption to grant the benefit of tax-exempt status to racially discriminatory educational entities, which "[exert] a pervasive influence on the entire educational process." Whatever may be the rationale for such private schools' policies, and however sincere the rationale may be, racial discrimination in education is contrary to public policy. Racially discriminatory educational institutions cannot be viewed as conferring a public benefit within the "charitable" concept discussed earlier. . . .

Petitioners contend that, even if the Commissioner's policy is valid as to nonreligious private schools, that policy cannot constitutionally be applied to schools that engage in racial discrimination on the basis of sincerely held religious beliefs. As to such schools, it is argued that the IRS construction of § 170 and § 501(c)(3) violates their free exercise rights under the Religion Clauses of the First Amendment. This contention presents claims not heretofore considered by this Court in precisely this context.

The governmental interest at stake here is compelling. . . . The Government has a fundamental, overriding interest in eradicating racial discrimination in education — discrimination that prevailed, with official approval, for the first 165 years of this Nation's constitutional history. That governmental interest substantially outweighs whatever burden denial of tax benefits places on petitioners' exercise of their religious beliefs. . . .

Bob Jones University also contends that denial of tax exemption violates the Establishment Clause by preferring religions whose tenets do not require racial discrimination over those which believe racial inter-mixing is forbidden. It is well settled that neither a state nor the Federal Government may pass laws which "prefer one religion over another," . . . but "[it] is equally true" that a regulation does not violate the Establish-ment Clause merely because it "happens to coincide or harmonize with the tenets of some or all religions." . . . The IRS policy at issue here is founded on a "neutral, secular basis," . . . and does not violate the Estab-lishment Clause. . . .

The judgments of the Court of Appeals are, accordingly, Affirmed.

10

CLARENCE HILLIARD

Down with the Honky Christ

January 30, 1976

White evangelicals were, for the most part, reluctant to support the civil rights movement. However, a handful of African Americans regularly challenged church leaders to take issues of race and justice more seriously. Among them was Chicago minister and National Association of Evan-gelicals activist Clarence Hilliard. This 1976 Christianity Today *article explains Hilliard's views.*

Most white people understand what a black person means when he calls someone a "honky." If they can't define it verbally they feel what it means — oppressor, bigot, slave-trader, exploiter, and in many ways, middle-class. A honky belongs to the status quo, the safe, the comfort-able. "Funky," on the other hand, may be a new term to many of you. In black parlance funky often has certain positive connotations. For example, if I call a song funky I mean that either voice or instrument

Clarence Hilliard, "Down with the Honky Christ—Up with the Funky Jesus," *Christianity Today*, January 30, 1976, 430–32.

stepped creatively from behind the strictures of the notes, boldly and freely authenticating his or her own soul in the rendition of the number. Funky stands opposite to honky—liberated, authentic, creative.

These two adjectives used in relation to the Gospel incarnate in Jesus pinpoint the problem I see in traditional evangelical circles, black or white. We and our leaders have been preaching a honky Christ to a world hungry for the funky Jesus of the Bible. The honky Christ stands with the status quo, the funky Jesus moves apart from the ruling religious system. Jesus stood with and for the poor and oppressed and disinherited. He came for the sick and needy.

Jesus announced his call in Luke 4:16–20. God's spirit was upon him "to preach good news to the poor. He has sent me to proclaim release to the captives and recovering of sight to the blind, to set at liberty those who are oppressed, to proclaim the acceptable year of the Lord." Nothing else is added to the call. He closed the book, gave it to the attendant, and sat down. And to ensure that his audience understood why he read that passage, he added, "Today this Scripture has been fulfilled in your hearing."

Christ never strayed from the focus of his call. When people questioned his messiahship such as John did in prison, Jesus confidently pointed to his work among the unloved: "the blind receive their sight and the lame walk, lepers are cleansed and the deaf hear, and the dead are raised up, and the poor hear good news."

Most Christian black theologians today would agree that ministry to the poor, the powerless, and the oppressed defines Christ's life on earth. The best adjective to describe it for me is funky, and the best symbol for his life is black. In our culture black has meant nigger, outcast, leper. In a way the Old Testament Hebrews were niggers. James Cone in *Black Theology and Black Power* approaches this when he says, "To be black means that your heart, your soul, your mind, and your body are where the dispossessed are." Black is the antithesis of white, and since the founding of our nation . . . black has symbolized the outsider.

If Christ was called to the poor and oppressed, as the Bible indicates, then that is also the call of his followers. And if black (or funky) is in our culture the most basic image for that group of people, then that call is to be black theologically. Someone has said that all persons seek to be equal to their superiors. That is the world's way; Christ's way is just the reverse. He came into the world as the ultimate "nigger" of the universe. He moved to the bottom of the social order, and his people and his culture rejected him. Christ's situation sounds like that of Any Black Person, Anywhere, U.S.A., giving added weight and validity to the symbol of a black Christ. In a deeper sense, however, Christ Jesus became blacker than black since "he was made sin for us." And he died on the cross, a death reserved for the niggers of his day. The system sought to lock him eternally in that despised, black status—damned forever.

Just as Jesus moved to the bottom of the social order, voluntarily giving up heaven for us, we as his followers are to move to the bottom of the social order—to become niggers with him. The black Christ calls the world to become black, to deny everything for what can only be a nigger's death—the cross. The black church sings a song like no one else: "Must Jesus bear the cross alone and all the world go free?" And we come back with, "No! There is a cross for everyone, and there is a cross for me." To be black theologically is to join yourself to Jesus and his cross.

Black Christians must consciously choose to be black. Our skin color does not automatically make us black theologically. The siren call of the system to move up the social ladder and out from among the poor means death. Theological blackness is a spiritual challenge for all, white and black. . . .

The challenge Jesus brings to white Christians is to deny their theological whiteness. Just as black is the best symbol for Jesus' ministry in our culture, so white or honky symbolizes what Jesus fought against. Theological whiteness frustrates and denies Christ's call and his methods. Each one of us is tempted to become white, as Moses (Heb. 11:24, 25) was tempted to remain within the Egyptian power structure.

If what I have described is the authentic call of Jesus through his Gospel, what is it that we evangelicals have been preaching? I said at the outset that we have been preaching a honky Christ to a hungry world. This honky Christ has no content; he does not come to the dispossessed. We preach a honky Christ of easy salvation. Specialists in getting quick, easy decisions for a strange, mystical, theologically white Christ are rapidly increasing. These persons peddle a Jesus easy to accept, a Jesus who demands very little commitment of energy, money, life.

The honky Jesus does not come down from heaven to the lowest social stratum, but grabs greedily upwards for the good things in life—at least that's the conclusion we could draw if we look at how some of his followers act. I seriously question the nebulous, almost contentless "Lord and *Saviour* Jesus Christ" present in some prominent evangelistic efforts. The Gospel, we are told, means personal salvation and little beyond that. We do not hear about Jesus' uncompromising commitment to liberation from all oppressive, satanic forces. The only cross in the honky gospel is the one on which Christ died. There is little mention of the crosses he carried before he shouldered the last one, or of the crosses he expects us to lift.

I sometimes get the impression that such an inoffensive Christ jumped off a mountain and impaled himself on the cross so that people could have someone to invite into their hearts as saviour. A person has only to pause, pray the prayer of faith, receive some minimal instruction, and then continue his life. The primary requirements for the new life shared with the new believers are: read your Bible, pray, attend church, and tell someone else about Christ. There is no call to feed the hungry and clothe the naked. The only call this gospel makes is to personal pietism. Sin, repentance, conversion, and the new life are dealt with almost exclusively in vertical dimensions. The horizontal dimensions of the Gospel are presented as optional, not intrinsic to it. . . .

When I say, "down with the honky Christ and up with the funky Jesus," then, I am suggesting not that we change Jesus but that we see him as he is. He moved creatively from behind the strictures of the religion of this day and obeyed God by serving the causes of justice, mercy, and faith. As his followers we dare not do less.

3

The Battle for the Schools

11

Engel v. Vitale *and the End of Official School Prayer*

1962

For decades Americans had debated what role religion should play in public education. Should class begin with prayer? Should the schools provide daily Bible reading? In 1962 the U.S. Supreme Court ruled in Engel v. Vitale *that mandatory classroom prayers violated the First Amendment's Establishment Clause. Justice Black's opinion is below. The next year, in* Abington School District v. Schempp, *the Court ruled that school-sponsored Bible reading in public schools was unconstitutional.*

Mr. Justice Black delivered the opinion of the Court.

The respondent Board of Education of Union Free School District No. 9, New Hyde Park, New York, acting in its official capacity under state law, directed the School District's principal to cause the following prayer to be said aloud by each class in the presence of a teacher at the beginning of each school day:

"Almighty God, we acknowledge our dependence upon Thee, and we beg Thy blessings upon us, our parents, our teachers and our Country."

This daily procedure was adopted on the recommendation of the State Board of Regents. . . .

Shortly after the practice of reciting the Regents' prayer was adopted by the School District, the parents of ten pupils brought this action in

---

Justice Hugo Black's Opinion re: *Engel v. Vitale* (1962). Available on LexisNexis.

a New York State Court insisting that use of this official prayer in the public schools was contrary to the beliefs, religions, or religious practices of both themselves and their children. Among other things, these parents challenged the constitutionality of both the state law authorizing the School District to direct the use of prayer in public schools and the School District's regulation ordering the recitation of this particular prayer on the ground that these actions of official governmental agencies violate that part of the First Amendment of the Federal Constitution which commands that "Congress shall make no law respecting an establishment of religion" — a command which was "made applicable to the State of New York by the Fourteenth Amendment of the said Constitution." . . .

We think that by using its public school system to encourage recitation of the Regents' prayer, the State of New York has adopted a practice wholly inconsistent with the Establishment Clause. There can, of course, be no doubt that New York's program of daily classroom invocation of God's blessings as prescribed in the Regents' prayer is a religious activity. It is a solemn avowal of divine faith and supplication for the blessings of the Almighty. . . .

The petitioners contend among other things that the state laws requiring or permitting use of the Regents' prayer must be struck down as a violation of the Establishment Clause because that prayer was composed by governmental officials as a part of a governmental program to further religious beliefs. For this reason, petitioners argue, the State's use of the Regents' prayer in its public school system breaches the constitutional wall of separation between Church and State. We agree with that contention since we think that the constitutional prohibition against laws respecting an establishment of religion must at least mean that in this country it is no part of the business of government to compose official prayers for any group of the American people to recite as a part of a religious program carried on by government. . . .

By the time of the adoption of the Constitution, our history shows that there was a widespread awareness among many Americans of the dangers of a union of Church and State. These people knew, some of them from bitter personal experience, that one of the greatest dangers to the freedom of the individual to worship in his own way lay in the Government's placing its official stamp of approval upon one particular kind of prayer or one particular form of religious services. They knew the anguish, hardship and bitter strife that could come when zealous religious groups struggled with one another to obtain the Government's stamp of approval from each King, Queen, or Protector that came to temporary power. The Constitution was intended to avert a part of this danger by leaving the government of this country in the hands of the people rather than in the hands of any monarch. But this safeguard was not enough. Our Founders were no more willing to let the content of their prayers and their privilege of praying whenever they pleased be influenced by the ballot box than they were to let these vital matters of personal conscience depend upon the succession of monarchs. The First Amendment was added to the Constitution to stand as a guarantee that neither the power nor the prestige of the Federal Government would be used to control, support or influence the kinds of prayer the American people can say—that the people's religions must not be subjected to the pressures of government for change each time a new political adminis-tration is elected to office. Under that Amendment's prohibition against governmental establishment of religion, as reinforced by the provisions of the Fourteenth Amendment, government in this country, be it state or federal, is without power to prescribe by law any particular form of prayer which is to be used as an official prayer in carrying on any pro-gram of governmentally sponsored religious activity. . . .

It has been argued that to apply the Constitution in such a way as to prohibit state laws respecting an establishment of religious services in public schools is to indicate a hostility toward religion or toward prayer. Nothing, of course, could be more wrong. The history of man is inseparable from the history of religion. And perhaps it is not too much to say that since the beginning of that history many people have devoutly believed that "More things are wrought by prayer than this world dreams of." It was doubtless largely due to men who believed this that there grew up a sentiment that caused men to leave the cross-currents of officially established state religions and religious persecu-tion in Europe and come to this country filled with the hope that they could find a place in which they could pray when they pleased to the God of their faith in the language they chose. And there were men of this same faith in the power of prayer who led the fight for adoption of our Constitution and also for our Bill of Rights with the very guarantees of religious freedom that forbid the sort of governmental activity which New York has attempted here. These men knew that the First Amend-ment, which tried to put an end to governmental control of religion and of prayer, was not written to destroy either. They knew rather that it was written to quiet well-justified fears which nearly all of them felt arising out of an awareness that governments of the past had shackled men's tongues to make them speak only the religious thoughts that govern-ment wanted them to speak and to pray only to the God that government wanted them to pray to. It is neither sacrilegious nor antireligious to say that each separate government in this country should stay out of the business of writing or sanctioning official prayers and leave that purely religious function to the people themselves and to those the people choose to look to for religious guidance.

12

TIM LAHAYE

A Christian View of Radical Sex Education

1969

Tim LaHaye is among the most influential evangelicals of the second half of the twentieth century. LaHaye served as the pastor of a San Diego megachurch; he established a Christian college; he helped found the Institute for Creation Research; and, with Jerry Falwell, he organized the Moral Majority. In the 1990s he coauthored the Left Behind series of books, which, with 80 million copies in print, are among the best-selling books in American history. In this 1969 document LaHaye expresses the concerns of many socially conservative ministers and parents about the implementation of new sex education curricula in the public schools.

Dear Parents:

As a parent, taxpayer, and a Christian, you need to be informed on the devastating Radical Sex Education Program now being advocated by some educators across America. It is so radical you have to read it to believe it. Most parents just can't believe intelligent, educated people would use the public schools to corrupt the morals of our children and young people.

From Tim LaHaye, *A Christian View of Radical Sex Education* (San Diego: Family Life Seminars, c. 1969), ii, 1–4, 6–9, 30–31, 40–43, 45–46.

In my opinion, if this material is made compulsory, it will corrupt the morals of our country in 10–15 years. Please read this booklet, and do what you can to oppose this dangerous practice. Most of those who are defending it don't really know what the material contains, or who is behind it.

Yours for a decent America,
Pastor Tim F. LaHaye

A Christian View of Sex Education

Contrary to popular opinion Christians are interested in Sex! Why shouldn't they be? Their Saviour Jesus Christ, the creator of all things was the originator of sex. The Bible is very clear on the subject, man was not complete without woman, and together they were given the greatest power on earth, the ability to create human life. (Gen. 2: 18–25.)

Christians are also interested in sex education! We know the importance of good education. Alter all, Christians were the guiding force behind practically all education in this country until the atheistic humanists under the guise of "Progressive Education" took over around the turn of the century. But we favor proper sex education with the Bible as our text. It is our conviction that the manufacturer of an item ought to be best qualified to instruct us on its use. Since God created man and sex, then it follows He is the best authority on how it should be used. . . .

Sex education to most people means "the birds and the bees" that we learned in school. The modern advocates of sex education are taking advantage of our old fashioned interpretation to propagate RADICAL SEX EDUCATION. As a Christian, if you look at the curriculum instead of the high sounding propaganda some educators put out about it you will find that it is really radical information that often borders on pornography and smut. It doesn't take the average parent, that investigates, very long to see that they are not talking about the birds and the bees but RADICAL SEX EDUCATION. . . .

At the risk of being branded a distributor of pornography, I am going to give you some examples of RADICAL SEX EDUCATION. Honestly, I would like to leave it out of the booklet entirely, but if I do, too many naive parents will accuse me of "much ado about nothing." We have come to respect educators so much in our country that we just can't conceive of their teaching anything that would not be in the best interest of our society. That is true of a large majority, and I would not cast an aspersion on them. Sad to say, it only takes one or two "bad apple" school teachers to spoil the publics' concept of the whole school house. Many schools seem to have one or two of the "bad apple" variety who become crusaders of RADICAL SEX EDUCATION. Frequently they are atheistic humanists with a prejudice against Christianity, religion and moral principles. Often they are profane, coarse individuals who are emotionally frustrated. In fact, some must be driven by a sadistic madness to destroy the innocence of the young people in their classrooms.

If you are too spiritually sensitive to read suggestive material, please skip this section. I would not like to be responsible for creating evil suggestions in the minds of my readers. If, however, you choose to read this section, please bear in mind that I am not using the worst material put out by these radical educators. I have some of their recommended course studies that my conscience will not permit me to have reprinted. . . .

At one private school, Mrs. Iseman watched a lecturer, using a plastic model, show high school students how to apply a contraceptive device. . . .

Since the entire progressive education system is based on the concept of "learning by doing" it doesn't take too much imagination to see how this kind of suggestive information put out by the "experts" fan the raging fires of teenage passion until they run the full orbit of the learning process.

One angry mother stated in a public meeting that her son's seventh grade teacher gave the assignment that each student was to ask his parents how frequently they had intercourse. This was to be reported and a graph was to be made of the results. I have a test given to the 10th grade class of the Loara High School of Anaheim, California in September of 1968. The test contains 30 yes or no questions and 51 matching terms questions. The crass frankness of these questions given on the 10th grade level are unbelievable. In fact, decency will not permit that I repeat them; however by selecting some of the terms provided to answer these questions you can easily see that the course that went before this test must have been an in depth study far beyond the need or mental requirement of 10th grade students. Consider some of the questions that would be required to give the following answers: "Promiscuity, Prophylactic, incest, adultery, homosexuality, syphilis, Lesbian, rape, transvestite, abortion, conception, arousal, chastity, climax, coitus, copulation, ejaculation, erection, frigidity, hymen, genitals, heterosexuality, mistress, venereal, prostitute and virgin." Is this what you send your young people to school to learn? . . .

SIECUS — The Source of Radical Sex Education

What seems like spontaneous sex education all across the United States isn't spontaneous at all — it is the result of a carefully laid plan by people whose objectives can scarcely be limited to education. This cleverly structed organization is called, by *McCall's* magazine, ". . . A high voltage, nonprofit organization called SIECUS, which is, without doubt the most important single force in sparking sex education in our schools. . . ." The National Education Association, that works very closely with SIECUS has this to say about them: "A new, voluntary, health agency, SIECUS (Sex Information and Education Council of the United States), has just been established in New York City. One of its many purposes will be to provide assistance to communities and schools wishing to embark on sex education programs. . . .

Pornography has always been profitable, but even that does not explain completely the purposes of the learned left wingers who make up SIECUS. The twisted minds of such people have an ulterior motive more important to them than money. They are bent on the degeneration of today's young people. . . .

Atheists tend to be amoral (there are some few exceptions). If a man does not believe in God he thinks he is free to lie, cheat, steal, ponder in pornography or do as he pleases with impunity. (He is wrong, of course, and one day he will give account to the God he deplores. But in the meantime he wrecks havoc on the souls, minds and bodies of men.)

The left wing atheist is not usually content to go his miserable way through life. Somehow he can't stand the sight of God fearing honest people who have a peace and joy in life he knows nothing about. Instead, he becomes an evangelist of Atheism. Another's faith is a sadistic challenge to him. Whether he realizes it or not, his efforts parallel the Communist, socialist and one world plotters. They are bent on the destruction of Christianity and all forms of religion — regardless the cost. It is no accident that many of the same people who worked so hard to drive the Bible out of our schools and secularize our society are the leaders of this nation wide RADICAL SEX EDUCATION movement.

Be sure of this, the RADICAL SEX EDUCATION program is an anti-God, anti-Christian and anti-Bible movement. It is time for Christians to stand up and lead our nation in a vigorous fight against this threat to our society. I am convinced there are enough moral minded people in our country that it can be done. SIECUS and their like are in the minority, but if we don't stop them soon they will turn our children into amoral images of themselves. . . .

It's time for Christian leaders across the land to mount a charge against this insidious cult of the pornographic. The Bible says, "Resist the Devil." Those who are ceaselessly working to destroy our children are certainly not inspired by God! So, ministers and Christians arise! Get involved in this fight to enslave the minds and bodies of our youth!

What Can We Do?

Although alarming, this dangerous high powered and RADICAL SEX EDUCATION movement can be stopped! Someone has said "to be forwarned is to be forarmed." Knowledge of the SIECUS subtleties is coming to light and the guns of opposition are being loaded. Traditionally, we Americans have regarded our children as our most treasured possession. If enough parents can be confronted with the facts they can mount a program of opposition that can drive SIECUS out of business, but it will take the active participation of millions of parents, working in their own community. Here are some suggestions for action.

1. Take a good look at the character building training you are providing for your children. If they are going to be able to stand against the flood tide of social chaos resulting from this RADICAL program they will need all the character training they can get.

   Do you see to it that your children go to a Bible teaching church regularly? Do you lead them in this practice? Have they personally received Jesus Christ as their Lord and Saviour? Have you? If not, they could already be on dangerous ground. The best defense against atheistic humanistic ideas is a vital belief in God through faith in His Son, Jesus Christ. The best preventive against your young people falling victim to the free love and other animal like notions of the SIECUS RADICALS is to dedicate their lives, body, soul and spirit to Jesus Christ "who loved them and gave himself for them." . . .

2. Take a careful look at what kind of sex education your young people are being taught in school. Be very thorough in your investigation, ask your children to tell you what they are learning and urge them to bring home materials used in class. Don't automatically assume that your school's sex education program is this new RADICAL SEX EDUCATION course of SIECUS. Give your principal the benefit of the doubt, he may be courageously opposing the administrative forces that are trying to make him use it. One high school principal I know, a fine Christian man,

said, "I would quit before I would permit that trash in our school!"

Such men need your support. . . . It's time for the silent majority to actively support those fine educators who are sincerely trying to do the best job they can to train our youth. Most of us have little knowledge of or appreciation for the powers and inner pressures on them.

Many schools still send home a slip asking for authorization for your children to attend sex education classes. Make sure you know what the course consists of before you sign it. Don't be afraid to ask to see the movie or filmstrip or to read the curriculum or have a friend or neighbor in whom you have confidence review it. If they are afraid to let you see it perhaps they have something to hide. . . .

3. You can alert many dedicated school teachers among your acquaintance of this dangerous form of education. I have found that the overwhelming majority of educators are very dedicated individuals and many are fine Christians. In our opposition to this RADICAL SEX EDUCATION we must be very careful not to alienate this majority group. They are often prone to be defensive the moment parents and tax payers begin to criticize the public schools. For that reason be very understanding and factual in presenting your case to them. . . .

4. If you find that your school is using RADICAL SIECUS approved materials, call for an appointment with your principal. It is possible he does not know the dangerous effects of this material nor the motives of those who have produced it. Kindly tell him your concern and urge him to read this booklet or other material at your disposal. If you can get him to quietly reject the SIECUS material you have done your community a great service. If he knows enough parents are concerned he may go back to the standard materials on sex education.

5. If you, like many parents, get nowhere with your principal, then you have to either get other parents concerned and organized or find such a group and join their vigorous campaigns. All community programs have to start with education. Whether you're starting a new group or joining one, the big job is to inform the parents in your community.

Order other copies of this booklet and get the parents to read it. . . .

6. Participate more in the election of school board officials. It
   ought to be instructive to concerned citizens that where school
   boards have Bible believing Christians in the majority on their
   boards, SIECUS has not been able to high pressure their school
   officials into adopting their course. Vigorously campaign for
   good replacements for school board members who back SIECUS
   materials.

   Too long we Christians have avoided politics calling it a "dirty
   business." This country was hammered out on the anvil of
   the Bible by predominately Christian men. The main problem
   with our country today is that Christians have retreated from
   politics. We need more Christians on every governmental level
   in this land! How can we be "salt" to the earth unless we get
   involved where the decisions are made?

   One thing needed in this country today is for qualified Christians to offer themselves to God for political leadership. It would
   be a wonderful thing if more than 50% of our leaders knew Jesus
   Christ and could pray to God through Him for wisdom. If that
   were the case we would see a deescalation of the amorality
   trends of today.

7. Write your President, Congressman and Senators. This is a national problem and they should be encouraged to stop the
   spending of federal monies for such pornographic education.
   Also urge them to get the Department of Health Education
   and Welfare to disapprove the SIECUS RADICAL SEX EDUCATION
   material.

8. Pray for this country! We are in serious trouble when these
   people can get into such high positions of leadership that they
   could prepare such morally degrading materials. If this country
   is ever to be saved it will have to be in answer to prayer.

13

The Benefits of Lynchburg Christian Academy
1975

This 1975 brochure for Jerry Falwell's Christian academy reflects the values that evangelical school administrators hoped to instill in their students. It also illustrates some of evangelicals' concerns about the American public school system and the youth culture of the time.

From "Five Things We Think You Will Like about Lynchburg Christian Academy," 1975, Lynchburg Christian Academy folder, Liberty University archives.

1 QUALITY EDUCATION. Students who graduate from Lynchburg Christian Academy receive a diploma from a fully accredited high school. Not only is Lynchburg Christian Academy accredited, but we feel that the curriculum is advanced significantly beyond the average public school in America.

2 NO DRUG PROBLEM. The drug abuse problem in our American schools is at epidemic stage today. Because our total faculty and administrative staff is composed of Christian people with high morals and standards, we are able to prevent such a drug problem at Lynchburg Christian Academy. This is not to say that no LCA student has ever used drugs. No school could make that statement in total honesty. However, we can say, to the best of our knowledge, we have no drug abuse problem.

3 BIBLE READING AND PRAYER ARE LEGAL AT LYNCHBURG CHRISTIAN ACADEMY. We have regular chapels in which we teach young people how to live by Biblical principles. Every day, young people are taught how to develop a personal relationship with Christ. The school is totally non-denominational and young people from all faiths attend. Over 700 are presently enrolled.

4 WE HAVE NO HIPPIES. Neatness of appearance, proper length of hair for boys, and right attitudes towards elders are all a part of our curriculum. We teach our young people to say "yes sir" and "no sir." Our students are taught the importance of dressing neatly and acceptably. They are also taught the "sacredness of hard work." Young people are no worse today than 25 years ago. They simply come from worse homes and schools. Proverbs 22:6 says "Train up a child in the way he should go; and when he is old, he will not depart from it."

5 OUR STUDENTS ARE TAUGHT TO LOVE AMERICA. Patriotism is a part of our program. Our students are taught to love this great nation and to respect her. We have never had an anti-American demonstration.

80

THERE ARE OTHER THINGS
YOU WILL LIKE ALSO —

We teach respect for parents. You can tell our boys from the girls without a medical examination. We teach our boys and girls to respect one another. Old-fashioned morality is taught and practiced. The use of alcoholic beverages and tobacco are not permitted by anyone. Our students are taught to take orders and respect authority.

81

14

PETER MARSHALL AND DAVID MANUEL

God in American History

1977

Many evangelicals believe that the United States, like ancient Israel, was a chosen nation divinely established by God to serve as his witness to humankind. Peter Marshall and David Manuel have popularized this view through their retelling of American history. Their books have become standard in conservative Christian schools and among homeschoolers around the country.

The Search

America, America—until about fifteen years ago, the name by itself would evoke a feeling of warmth. Whether it was pride or gratitude or hope, the response of the majority of people on earth was deeply positive. America's moral and fiscal currency was the soundest in the world; you could bank on it, and most of the world did. Abroad, we were the free world's policeman; an encouraging older brother to those young nations struggling to achieve democracy; and the hope of all peoples still in bondage. In general, we were the most steadying influence on an uneasy globe. And at home, we were supremely confident that we were indeed making the world a better place to live in. We believed that technologically and diplomatically, it was only a matter of time before this assignment would be satisfactorily completed.

America itself already *was* a better place to live. . . . In a word, *optimism* summed up America. The American Dream was about to come true.

And then, with a suddenness that is still bewildering, everything went out of balance. Our military ventures ceased to go according to the script. And our young President, the personification of The Dream, was

From Peter Marshall and David Manuel, *The Light and the Glory* (Old Tappan, N.J.: Revell, 1977), 13–20, 22–26.

assassinated. Our young people began to revolt on a scale that no generation ever had before—indiscriminately lashing out at all authority or escaping into the mindless self-destruction of drug abuse. The emerging nations, to whom we had given so freely, were almost unanimous in their hatred of us. Our foreign policy devolved into one, of *re*action, rather than action; in effect, we *had* no foreign policy.

Domestically, our economy waxed increasingly erratic; economists could no longer predict its gyrations, let alone do anything to stabilize it. Our children's mathematics and English aptitudes were plummeting; by college-entrance standards they were two years behind the averages of a decade before. . . .

But perhaps the most mystifying indicator of all was the loss of moral soundness. . . .

And yet, the sexual promiscuity, which we scrambled to accommodate through legalized abortion, permissive sex education, and ever more effective birth preventatives, was not in itself the most telling sign of the depth of the moral decay. Nor was it the dis-integration of the family unit, the common thread which was all that was keeping the fabric of America from coming apart at the seams. . . .

The most significant index of the extent of our moral decay was our very indifference to it. Pornography had insinuated itself into practically every level of our daily life, including our language. Corrupt personal and business practices which once would have erupted into major scandals, today seemed scarcely scandalous. But where once we would have been up in arms, speaking out, writing letters, and voting, now we just shook our heads and counted it as another sign of the times. . . .

What *had* happened to The Dream? . . . Our best thinkers could not come up with any conclusive answers, and many Americans gave up asking what had happened.

And yet, this book has an answer. To many, the answer will be incredible, even preposterous, although two hundred years ago, the majority of Americans would have accepted it readily enough. And a hundred and fifty years before that, for the first settlers who found their way to these shores, it would have been the *only* answer.

Night had fallen on the small New England harbor, and the fishing boats rocked gently at anchor. Inside the nearby chapel, a gathering of some two hundred people was illuminated by electric candles which glowed softly against the wood paneling. The speaker came quickly to the heart of his message: "This nation was founded by God with a special calling. The people who first came here knew that they were being led here by the Lord Jesus Christ, to found a nation where men, women, and children were to live in obedience to Him . . . This was truly to be *one nation under God.*"

The speaker paused. "The reason, I believe, that we Americans are in such trouble today is that we have forgotten this. We've rejected it. In fact, we've become quite cynical about it. We, as a people, have thrown away our Christian heritage."

That was a strong statement; would he be able to back it up? One of the listeners in the audience wondered what exactly our Christian heritage *was*—and had wondered it before: four years before, to be exact. The listener was David Manuel, who, while an editor at a major New York publishing house, had discovered to his dumbfoundment that God was real. . . .

The speaker was Peter Marshall, who had grown up in rebellion against the spiritual legacy of two famous Christian parents: the late Chaplain of the Senate, also named Peter, and his author-wife Catherine. . . .

What made the nation's need even more compelling, he said, was the realization of how much God's hand had played a part not only in America's founding, but, indeed, in its very discovery.

"I want to read to you what Christopher Columbus himself said about why he came here." Peter began to quote to the audience a few translated excerpts from an obscure volume of Columbus's which had never previously appeared in English.

It was the Lord who put into my mind (I could feel his hand upon me) the fact that it would be possible to sail from here to the Indies. All who heard of my project rejected it with laughter, ridiculing me. There is no question that the inspiration was from the Holy Spirit, because He comforted me with rays of marvelous inspiration from the Holy Scriptures . . . .

Stunned amazement swept the chapel audience. Did Columbus really think that way? All we had ever read or been taught had indicated that Columbus discovered the New World by accident, while seeking a trade route to the Indies. No mention had ever been made of his faith, let alone that he felt he had been given his life's mission directly by God. Nor had we suspected that he felt called to bear the Light of Christ to undiscovered lands in fulfillment of biblical prophecy, or that he had been guided by the Holy Spirit every league of the way—and knew it.

Moreover, this was not the wishful thinking of some overly enthusiastic fundamentalist; *these were Columbus's own words*—words that few Americans had ever read before they had appeared in the article Peter had quoted. To David, seated in the audience, the impact of this revelation was staggering. For the thought suddenly occurred to him: *What if God had conceived a special plan for America?*

What if Columbus's discovery had not been accidental at all? What if it were merely the opening curtain of an extraordinary drama . . . ? Hadn't Peter just referred to the first settlers as having been called by God to found a Christian nation?

Did God have a plan for America? Like all those who have discovered the reality of the living Christ, we knew that God had a plan for each individual's life—a plan which could, with spiritual effort, be discerned and followed. *What if He dealt with whole nations in the same way?*

The Bible said He did, of course; that the Jews were His chosen people, and that, if they would obey His commandments, He would bless them *as a nation. . . .*

Many modern Christians believe that this idea of a corporate covenant relationship ceased with the coming of Jesus Christ. They feel that, with the advent of Christianity, man's relationship to his God became an individualized and highly personal matter.

But what if God's point of view had never changed? What if, in addition to the intimate relationship with the individual through Jesus Christ the Saviour, God continued to deal with nations corporately, as He had throughout Old Testament history? What if, in particular, He had a plan for those He would bring to America, a plan which saw this continent as the stage for a new act in the drama of mankind's redemption? Could it be that we Americans, as a people, were meant to be a "light to lighten the Gentiles" (Luke 2:32)—a demonstration to the world of how God intended His children to live together under the Lordship of Christ? Was our vast divergence from this blueprint, after such a promising beginning, the reason why we now seem to be heading into a new dark age?

It all seemed pretty fantastic, but as David and Peter talked about it after the meeting that night, the whole hypothesis became more and more plausible. And so, one sunny May morning in 1975, they—we—were on our way to Boston to ascertain whether research would bear out these ideas—possibly even provide enough evidence for a book. . . .

It became clear to us that here we were indeed onto something—that there had been others who had felt that God did have a specific and unique plan for America. . . . The first settlers consciously thought of themselves as a people called into a continuation of the covenant relationship with God and one another which Israel had entered into.

We later discovered that they even felt that passages in the Bible . . . (originally addressed to Israel) applied in particular to them. . . .

Furthermore, they saw themselves as called into their new Promised Land in order to found a new Israel, which would be a light to the whole world. "A city set upon a hill" was how John Winthrop, the first Governor of Massachusetts, put it. . . .

In truth, this book is not intended to be a history textbook, but rather a search for the hand of God in the different periods of our nation's beginnings. We feel, due to the extreme gravity of America's present spiritual and moral condition, that it is imperative that we Americans rediscover our spiritual moorings. . . .

Our basic presupposition—that God had a definite and extremely demanding plan for America—was confirmed, albeit in a number of surprising ways. Men like Columbus turned out to be far more dedicated to God's service than we had imagined. Others, like Thomas Jefferson, whom we had assumed to be reasonably devout, turned out to be quite the opposite.

Once it had become clear that God did have a plan for America, our search for evidence of this plan became akin to tracking a rich vein of gold through a mountain. The vein of gold had four main characteristics.

First, God had put a specific "call" on this country and the people who were to inhabit it. In the virgin wilderness of America, God was making His most significant attempt since ancient Israel to create a new Israel of people living in obedience to the laws of God, through faith in Jesus Christ. . . .

A new Jerusalem, a model of the Kingdom of Christ upon earth—we Americans were intended to be living proof to the rest of the world that it *was* possible to live a life together which reflected the Two Great Commandments and put God and others ahead of self.

Second, this call was to be worked out in terms of the settlers' covenant with God, and with each other. Both elements of this covenant—the vertical relationship with God, and the horizontal relationship with their fellowmen—were of the utmost importance to the early comers (as the first Christian settlers called themselves). Concerning the vertical aspect of the covenant, they saw no delineation between the two Testaments, believing that an unchanging God had written them both. They saw themselves as being called into a direct continuation of the covenant relationship between God and Abraham. . . .

And as each church-community grew and became, in effect, a town, these covenants provided the pattern for the first successful civil governments in the western hemisphere. Historians and sociologists alike have long regarded the early New England town meetings as the purest and most successful form that democracy has ever taken. But few, if any, have acknowledged what lay at the core of *how* and *why* they worked so well. There would be many modifications, but American democracy owes its inception to the covenants of the first churches on her shores.

God did keep His end of the bargain (which is the third major theme), and He did so on both an individual and a corporate basis. It is a sobering experience to look closely at our history and see just how highly God regarded what can only be called "a right heart attitude." One finds long droughts broken by a settlement's deliberately fasting and humbling itself, turning back to the God whom they once trusted and had imperceptibly begun to take for granted. One also finds instances of one settlement being spared from Indian attack, while another is decimated, when the only apparent difference seemed to be in their heart attitude towards God and one another. . . .

The key, of course, was that His people—three thousand years ago, three hundred years ago, or today—had to first see that they were sinners. Without accepting that truth, there could be no repentance, for they would not see any need for humbling themselves. This was the linchpin to God's plan for America: that we see ourselves, individually and corporately, in a state of continuing need of God's forgiveness, mercy, and support. And this was the secret of the horizontal aspect of the covenant as well: for only at the foot of the Cross can we be truly united in Christ. Only starting from that position of each of us having to see our own sin, can we be truly one in the Spirit.

And incidentally, from *this* position, it is impossible to enter into nationalistic pride. Inherent in God's call upon our forefathers to found a Christian nation was the necessity to live in a state of constant need and dependency upon His grace and forgiveness. Anyone tempted today to take an elitist attitude regarding our nation's call need only look at how badly we have failed—and continue to fail—to live up to God's expectations for us.

Yet in the early days of our history, it is astonishing to see how few people it took to begin a cycle of repentance, followed by the return of God's grace. And so, this was the final major theme we found: that when a group of people, no matter how small or ordinary, was willing to die out to their selfish desires, *the life which came out of that death was immeasurable, and continued to affect lives far into the future.* This was especially true of the leaders God raised up for these early settlers. Men like Bradford, Winthrop, and Washington, instead of aspiring to greatness (which is so often the goal today), truly wanted nothing more than to serve God's people. And because these servant-leaders were living out the example of Jesus Christ, who said, "I am among you as one who serves," God was able to use them mightily to show the way in the building of His new Promised Land.

15

DUANE GISH

Dinosaurs and Young-Earth Creationism

1977

Many evangelicals have long believed that Darwinian theories of evolution contradict the Bible. In 1970 a few prominent leaders established the Institute for Creation Research with the goal of undertaking and promoting credible scientific research to substantiate the Genesis account of creation and a "young" earth, and to refute evolutionary theory. Duane Gish was one of the institute's leaders. This selection, taken from a children's picture book about dinosaurs, illustrates the views of a prominent creationist. Books like this have provided curricula for the growing evangelical and homeschooling movements.

Where did dinosaurs come from? How long ago did they roam ancient swamps upon the earth? What did they look like? Whatever became of them? These are some of the questions we will try to answer in this book.

Where Did Dinosaurs Come From?

There is a difference of opinion among scientists on this question. . . .

Some scientists, who are evolutionists, believe that dinosaurs evolved (slowly came into being by many in-between forms) from some kind of ancient reptile about 200 million years ago, and that they became extinct (died out) about 70 million years ago. . . .

There are other scientists, called creationists, who believe that the scientific evidence shows that dinosaurs did not evolve, but that they

From Duane Gish, *Dinosaurs: Those Terrible Lizards* (San Diego: Creation-Life Publishers, 1977), 9, 12–13, 15–16, 56–57, 59–60.

were created by God, just as described in the Bible. Creationists believe that dinosaurs were created the same time that Man and all other creatures were created, probably sometime less than 10,000 years ago. . . .

The Bible tells us that God made Man and the dinosaurs (included among the beasts of the earth) on the sixth day of creation. . . .

Is there scientific evidence that Man and dinosaurs lived at the same time?

Yes! Although the bones of dinosaurs have not yet been found together with those of Man, their footprints have.

In the rocky bottom of the Paluxy River near Glen Rose, Texas, dinosaur and human footprints have been found together.

In at least one case, a human footprint had been made directly on top of a dinosaur footprint.

Evidently some people had walked (or run!) through a muddy area about the same time dinosaurs were walking (or running!) through this area. The mud quickly hardened, and soon afterwards the footprints were covered with soil, brought in apparently by a flood. Before very long, everything became very hard, turning into rock.

Thousands of years later, local flooding had eroded (washed away) the soil and rock on top to uncover these footprints once more. This was possible because the rocky material which covered the footprints was softer and more easily eroded than the rock in which the footprints were made.

Although Man and the dinosaurs were probably afraid of each other, and so usually stayed away from one another, these footprints show that there were times, perhaps during emergencies, when their paths did cross.

The Bible gives us some other clues that Man and the dinosaurs lived at the same time, for in the Book of Job we find a pretty good description of a dinosaur, indicating that people in those ancient days, after the great Flood of Noah, still remembered dinosaurs.

Whatever Became of the Dinosaurs?

This is the question scientists have thought a lot about but have never really been able to answer. All kinds of ideas have been suggested, but none of them seem to fit all the facts. Nobody really knows why all the dinosaurs became extinct (died out). We don't know either, but we may have a good idea.

Some scientists have suggested that the dinosaurs, with their tiny brains, couldn't compete with the much more intelligent mammals. . . .

Others have suggested that egg-eating mammals ate so many dinosaur eggs that dinosaurs died off much faster than they were being born, and so they finally died out completely. . . .

Various other ideas have been suggested to explain the death of all the dinosaurs, such as disease, glandular trouble, cosmic rays from the explosion of a star (supernova), and changes in the magnetic field of the earth. None of these ideas seem to be scientifically reasonable.

The idea suggested most often by scientists to explain the extinction of dinosaurs is the suggestion that the weather all over the earth changed so drastically that the dinosaurs simply could no longer survive in this 'new' world. Perhaps the lush, plenteous vegetation that covered much of the earth at that time disappeared. This caused the plant-eating dinosaurs to die out. The meat-eating dinosaurs then died out because they had no plant-eating dinosaurs to eat.

We believe this to be a very reasonable explanation. . . .

But what happened? What happened to change the climate all over the world so drastically? What could have happened to change Greenland from a beautiful, warm, green, tropical paradise into a frozen wasteland, and the lovely green Arctic and Antarctic areas into lands of perpetual ice? What happened to the climate of the world that changed the playlands of the dinosaurs in China and Utah into deserts? What caused the Ice Age?

A lot of ideas have been suggested, but when all is said and done, scientists have to admit that they really don't know. We can't really say we know either, because we weren't there when all this happened. We believe we have a pretty good idea, however, what happened to the earth to make the weather change so drastically. We believe the Bible gives us the answer.

In the Book of Genesis the Bible tells us about a great flood that covered the entire earth and wiped out all people and land animals, except those on the Ark. It was this flood, or what caused the flood, that changed the climate of the earth. How did it do that?

Water vapor is water in the form of an invisible gas; like that, for instance, which collects on the outside of an ice-cold glass of water. We have rain when water vapor in the sky (atmosphere) condenses (forms moisture or droplets of water) and falls down to the ground.

If all the water vapor now in the atmosphere of the earth condensed and fell in the form of rain over the entire surface of the earth, only about one inch of rain would fall and then there would be no water vapor left. The atmosphere would be bone-dry. This would be true, of course, only if the rain covered the *entire* earth.

The Bible tells us, however, that it rained very hard over the entire earth for at least forty days and forty nights during the great flood of Noah. This would bring down many, many inches of rain. The Bible also talks about the breaking up of the great deep. This means the crust of the earth broke up. Probably, as a result, the land sank down and the ocean floors came up (perhaps even large continents broke up to make smaller ones!). All of this along with the rain caused all of the land to be flooded by water. Even the highest mountains were covered.

If there is only enough water vapor in the atmosphere today for one inch of rain to fall (this would last only about one hour), but it rained hard for forty days and forty nights during the flood, there had to be a lot more water vapor in the atmosphere before the flood than after the flood. Because of this, the weather would have been much warmer before the flood than after the flood. Why do we say this?

Water vapor absorbs and helps to hold in the heat from the sun. When the atmosphere has a lot of water vapor in it, it is warmer than when it has very little. Therefore, the atmosphere before the flood, which had a lot of water vapor, would have absorbed and held more heat from the sun than does our atmosphere today, which has much less water vapor. This would have made the earth warmer than it is today, because the warm atmosphere would have acted like a warm blanket.

Because of this big change in atmospheric conditions at the time of the flood, the world became drier and cooler. The North and South Poles became lands of perpetual ice, and Greenland changed from a tropical paradise to a frozen wasteland. Lands that had been lush and green turned into deserts. The oceans became cooler.

As a result of this change in the earth, the dinosaurs (and many other creatures such as the flying reptiles and the sea reptiles) all died out. None are still alive today. All we have left today to tell us about dinosaurs are their fossil bones, fossil footprints, and fossil eggs.

But what an exciting story these dinosaur fossils tell us! Don't you agree that it is a lot of fun reading and thinking about dinosaurs?

Are you sad that they are all gone?

Maybe we should be glad.

Tyrannosaurus!

Brrrrrrrr!!

4

Focusing on the Family

16

CARL F. H. HENRY

Abortion: An Evangelical View

February 1971

Historians have debated when and to what extent evangelicals rose up against the practice and legalization of abortion. It is clear from this document, published two years before the Roe v. Wade *decision, that some leading evangelicals had strong opinions regarding the move to liberalize the nation's abortion laws. Its author, Carl F. H. Henry, served as the first editor-in-chief of* Christianity Today. *His many publications helped shape the modern evangelical movement.*

In five short years the long-taboo subject of abortion, once mainly catalogued with family disgrace or tragedy, has become a matter of wide public discussion. As a result abortion in America changed from an abhorrent to a welcomed alternative. In ancient times, a morally insensitive age when fathers left unwanted baby girls to die on the public garbage heaps, primitive Christianity sharply disapproved of infanticide. Even the Islamic Koran forbade the killing of infant girls.

Now at a time when, under paganizing pressures, civil law accommodates discretionary infanticide, too many churchmen are prone to approve abortion as something outside the scope of Christian ethics.

Carl F. H. Henry, "Abortion: An Evangelical View," *Christian Heritage*, February 1971, 22–25.

Their assumption, however, merely echoes the superficial judgment of those outside of the church and therefore lacks Christian credibility. . . .

I maintain that abortion is not a completely private medical problem, any more than pollution of the environment can be dismissed as a purely chemical problem. But the Church is surely in no enviable position, whatever her attitude toward abortion, if she relies mainly upon legal measures to shape human conduct and lacks rational persuasion and moral example to challenge the mind and will of the masses to pursue what is right.

Ecclesiastical concern has focused so intently on the liberalization of state laws that the public is made to feel that the abortion-problem is best solved by getting rid of the laws which supposedly create it, a greater evil than abortion itself. . . .

For those sufficiently aligned with the Bible to be Protestant evangelicals, Roman Catholics and Orthodox Jews, the matter of abortion cannot be settled quite so simply; abortion, after all, is not only of physical and legal interest but equally a spiritual and moral concern.

In some circles abortion is already being hailed as the number one method of birth control. . . .

Numerous professional groups and conferences are coming out in favor of abortion. The clergy have become a vanguard among them. The committee report on sex accepted by the General Assembly for study in the United Presbyterian Church in the U.S.A. recommends removing abortion from legal answerability and making it solely a matter of personal decision between the mother, her physician, and her pastor or counselor. By a narrow nine-vote margin the General Assembly ruled that adultery, prostitution, fornication and homosexuality are sin; it did not designate abortion under any circumstances to be such. The General Conference of the United Methodist Church of 1970 urged "that states remove the regulation of abortion from the criminal code, placing it instead under regulations relating to other procedures of standard medical practice." . . .

Conditions under which abortion has previously been considered moral are for the most part clear-cut: when pregnancies are induced by rape or incest; when physicians, psychologists or psychiatrists approve abortion as therapeutic; and possibly when serious mental or physical deformity are in prospect for the fetus. . . .

If abortion is completely and only a medical matter, as is now often claimed, it should nonetheless be obvious that most abortions today are not really sought for exclusively medical reasons; sometimes no medical reason whatever is involved. Sound medical reasons were stipulated by the long-established laws that accommodated abortion. Precisely these laws, however, are now under fire. The reasons for abortion increasingly turn out to be neither moral nor medical reasons at all, but rather, social rationalization and private preference.

This is quite clear from the hurried way in which moderns dismiss the question of when the fetus becomes a person. When does life become human? The Methodist Board of Social Concerns has committed itself to the so-called "tissue theory" according to which "the fetus is not a person, but rather tissue with the potentiality, in most cases, for becoming a person" (Statement on Responsible Parenthood, adopted Oct. 8, 1969).

Such thinking is as far removed as it can possibly be from the traditional Roman Catholic view that human life exists from the moment of conception, and that abortion is therefore murder at any stage whatever at which life is forming within the mother's body. The tissue theory, on the other hand, implies that a life becomes human only when viable outside the mother's womb, and not before the doctor at delivery spanks the baby's bottom. The traditional Jewish view, it may be noted, was that nascent life becomes human at birth; for all that, Jewry regarded the fetus with holy awe and acknowledged God to be the sovereign opener of the womb. . . .

At stake is the question whether a human life is being deliberately prematurely delivered in order to destroy it. If the fetus is prematurely taken from the womb, moreover, at a stage when its life could be nurtured for development into normal childhood, can such deliberate destruction of life be anything other than immoral? To be sure, this issue is not the only moral or spiritual question involved in abortion; the question, however, whether we are tolerating the murder of a brother is one that no society interested in human and minority rights dare ignore. To say that a baby has no right to life if it is unwanted skirts the real issue from God's point of view; does not the fetus have the right to be wanted? Has the fetus at no stage prior to delivery any rights of its own? . . .

Is the life of a helpless fetus forfeitable simply because the mother wills its death and the parents sense no Good Samaritan obligation to spare it? If so, do the mother and father in principle forfeit any rights of their own when they become senile and their children are disposed to put them out of the way? If the decision to preserve or destroy a living fetus lacking full human life rests upon a parent's personal convenience or upon social considerations such as the population explosion, is not the case even stronger then for a child to dispose of parents when senility overtakes them? If we are free to destroy human life and to deny its dignity at one stage, why not at another?

If, on the other hand, the unborn child has personal rights even before delivery, and if its right to be born has public implications, then the human self is entitled to protection even when it cannot protect itself. The right of the weak and helpless to protection and mercy has always been a distinctive emphasis of Christian morality; reverence for life even at its despised frontiers and not merely at its most cherished horizons was an apostolic virtue.

With no persuasive reasons for considering abortion to be just or compassionate, how can we escape the verdict that abortion is in many, if not most, instances today a lapse of Twentieth Century feticide or infanticide? . . .

While case studies show that most women who undergo abortions experience no physical harm, these studies cannot confirm the presumption that bearing the child would have produced psychological aberration. . . . And how often are a mother's secret guilt-feelings actually brought to light? Is there never a moment when she asks: "Did I kill my baby?" . . .

The connection between easy abortion and sexual promiscuity is obvious. While married women seeking abortions once outnumbered unwed girls four to one, the ratio is now thought to be about equally balanced. About one in ten women wanting abortions blame birth control failure for their pregnancies; most such failure involve married women who are less sophisticated about contraceptive techniques than their unmarried sisters. Yet for all their know-how, modern teen-agers face a rising problem of unwanted pregnancies. The ages at which premarital intercourse is ventured and at which unwanted pregnancies occur are falling lower and lower. The problem of the unwanted child is especially acute on college and university campuses, however, where intellectual criteria are presumed to count for something. . . .

A Christian response to the abortion-crisis encourages a new respect and sense of responsibility for the body and its use. A woman's body is not the domain and property of others. It is hers to control, and she alone is responsible to God and to society, for its use. When she yields that control, and through pregnancy is involved in intrapersonal relationships with a second party, and through conception to a third party, and indeed to human society as a whole, it becomes too late for her to justify abortion on the basis of self-determination. The God of creation and redemption is also the guardian of the womb, however much abortion-on-demand would contradict or scorn such a conviction. In abortion-on-demand one's own private decision determines the ordering of human life. Obviously such self-autonomy cannot be maximized, however, for even were suicide-on-demand to follow, there remains at last a final judgment by the Lord and Giver of Life.

17

The House Debates "Pro-Life" Civil Disobedience
1985, 1986

With the right to abortion protected at least in the early stages of pregnancy, increasing numbers of evangelicals and Catholics began to use civil disobedience to try to stop the practice. Occasionally their actions turned violent. This congressional hearing lays out many of the issues at stake. The key witness, Roman Catholic Joseph Scheidler, was one of the founding fathers of the "pro-life" movement. He influenced many evangelical activists.

Statement of Joseph M. Scheidler, Executive Director, Pro-Life Action League

Mr. SCHEIDLER. Mr. Chairman and members of this subcommittee, I am Joseph Scheidler, the executive director of the Pro-Life Action League headquartered in Chicago. My organization is representative of hundreds of prolife groups throughout this country working through legal, nonviolent, direct action to stop the destruction of human lives by abortion.

In Chicago our efforts resulted in closing six abortion chambers. . . .

Other abortion facilities around the country have been closed through nonviolent direct action. The lives of many unborn children and their mothers have been saved through sidewalk counseling. One day

Abortion Clinic Violence: Oversight Hearings before the Subcommittee on Civil and Constitutional Rights of the Committee on the Judiciary, House of Representatives, March 6, 12, April 3, 1985, and December 17, 1986. Washington, D.C.: U.S. Government Printing Office, http://catalog.hathitrust.org/Record/003491171.

in Chicago 20 women were talked out of having their abortions at one clinic on Michigan Avenue. In Chicago alone we have been able to prevent, through our peaceful persuasion, some 2,000 abortions each year.

Abundant scientific evidence proves that human life does begin with fertilization and that any attack, we believe, on this life is tantamount to murder. The abortionists know the biological facts and routinely attest to these.

The 1973 Supreme Court abortion ruling ignored the question of the beginning of human life. It made abortion legal for the full term of pregnancy, based on a privacy right that it could not find in the document it used to justify its ruling. This ruling did not change the fact that abortion is wrong. . . .

Any nation that destroys its posterity at such a rapid rate cannot survive. The unborn child deserves both dignity and protection. No Supreme Court can remove that dignity or its humanity. No semantics can rob him or her of the right to life nor consign them to the scrap heap and make their killing right. . . .

We have no intention of being intimidated by threats to our rights of free speech, assembly, or redress of grievances. We will return again and again to the abortuaries to talk women out of abortions, to try to convert medical personnel who have turned their healing profession into a killing profession. We will confront in the courts and on the streets every false arrest, every malicious prosecution, and every unconstitutional injunction attacking our first amendment rights.

We are aware of attacks against abortion facilities. Knowing what takes place inside the abortion chambers, we understand the moral outrage at the waste of human life that prompts this response. Some have condemned the destruction of abortion facilities. The Pro-Life Action League and others refuse to condemn it because we refuse to cast the abortionists in the role of victim when they are, in fact, victimizers.

No one has been killed or injured in the attacks on abortion facilities, but thousands of human lives are destroyed inside these buildings every day. Those of us who place greater value on human life than on real estate will condemn the destruction of brick and mortar when the abortionists condemn the destruction of our little brothers and sisters. . . .

As activists we caution the abortionists and those defending their lethal trade to cease their campaign to deny us our constitutional rights. Nonviolent direct action to end abortion is preferable to bombing abortion chambers, but if access to free speech, assembly, and redress of grievances are denied, the violence of abortion will inevitably be opposed by other means. Our methods are open and above board. Our abortion clinic sit-ins are within the law, in light of the common law defense of necessity. . . .

Mrs. SCHROEDER. Thank you for being here, sir. I have some questions.

My understanding is, and maybe it's wrong, but that you have advocated followers to go into clinics, posing as patients, and then begin shouting slogans, linking arms to block off labs and procedure rooms. Now, do you think that is legal?

Mr. SCHEIDLER. That is some kind of a mutation. We do go into clinics. We do pose as patients and we talk to the patients inside the clinic. If we have a sit-in we will go into the clinic, obviously, for a sit-in. We don't mix the two. . . .

We are trying to save human lives, and sometimes to—

Mrs. SCHROEDER. But do you think your cause, then, is higher than the law?

Mr. SCHEIDLER. Yes.

Mrs. SCHROEDER. That's what you're saying.

Mr. SCHEIDLER. Yes. . . .

Believe me, sometimes when you're in a pitched conversation or battle in front of a clinic there are some heated words. I don't condone that. But I don't think it is nearly as important as the fact that this woman is taking a child in there to have its arms and legs pulled off, be disemboweled and have its brains sucked out.

Mrs. SCHROEDER. Sir, . . . you are making value judgments about women walking into these clinics who could be in life-threatening positions. . . .

I really resent the fact that you think women go walking in for abortions just like they're getting their hair done. It's a very, very heavy decision.

Mr. SCHEIDLER. Why is it so heavy? . . .

Mrs. SCHROEDER. I know that I have overextended my time, but I just really feel that we have established one thing, and that is that you really do feel trespassing and things like that are OK—

Mr. SCHEIDLER. Yes, that's right— . . .

Mrs. SCHROEDER. But don't you think a woman—

Mr. SCHEIDLER. She rarely has a life-threatening situation when she goes into an abortion clinic.

Mrs. SCHROEDER. Well, but the woman happens to be, I think, still a human being. We still classify them that way.

Mr. SCHEIDLER. So is the baby.

Mrs. SCHROEDER. They may not have equal rights in this country, but we are still classified, I think, as human beings.

Mr. SCHEIDLER. But her life is not at stake.

Can't you understand the difference, the distinction?

Mrs. SCHROEDER. Sir, I resent that very much, and I want to tell you why. OK?

Mr. SCHEIDLER. Well, you said it.

Mrs. SCHROEDER. Can I tell you why?

Mr. SCHEIDLER. Yeah.

Mrs. SCHROEDER. I have had two children, I have lost two children, and it is not an easy thing for me to talk about.

Mr. SCHEIDLER. Then you should be prolife.

Mrs. SCHROEDER. I am prolife, sir—

Mr. SCHEIDLER [continuing]. Of defending the killing of children.

Mrs. SCHROEDER. But I could be in a very threatening situation if I were pregnant again. And I resent your sitting there saying to me that women just deal with this lightly. We don't.

Mr. SCHEIDLER. I never said that.

Mrs. SCHOEDER. Well, you are implying that, sir.

Mr. SCHEIDLER. I'm implying that you think it's a serious decision. Then why is it a serious decision?

Mrs. SCHROEDER. I'm saying it is a very serious decision.

Mr. SCHEIDLER. Why?

Mrs. SCHROEDER. Women walking into those clinics are under tremendous stress—

Mr. SCHEIDLER. Why?

Mrs. SCHROEDER [continuing]. And you only intimidate them more.

Mr. SCHEIDLER. Why?

Mrs. SCHROEDER. Because they're trying to deal with their situation, with the child's situation, and it is tough. And it is not something where someone needs to be yelling "murderer" at them. Under the law they are not considered a murderer, under many religions certainly not. . . .

Mr. SCHUMER [continuing]. In your interchange with Mrs. Schroeder, you said God has said they are children. You and I are of different religions. My God doesn't say that.

Are you telling me that the United States of America ought to impose the view of your God upon me and my family?

Mr. SCHEIDLER. I believe in one God.

Mr. SCHUMER. So, you believe my God has to be your God.

Mr. SCHEIDLER. I believe our God has to be the God that—

Mr. SCHUMER. Let's say I don't believe in one God.

Mr. SCHEIDLER. Then you're wrong.

Mr. SCHUMER. I'm wrong.

What should be done to force me to believe in your God?

Mr. SCHEIDLER. Well, maybe you need some education on the existence of God and scripture and the fact that God, himself, says, "The Lord, your God, is one God."

Mr. SCHUMER. Should I believe in Christ?

Mr. SCHEIDLER. I think you should.

Mr. SCHUMER. Would you want to pass laws saying that I should?

Mr. SCHEIDLER. No.

Mr. SCHUMER. No.

And now I want you to tell me the difference between not passing laws to do that but passing laws as you advocate on this issue, because they are exactly the same, they're religious beliefs.

Mr. SCHEIDLER. They're not exactly the same. . . .

Mr. EDWARDS. Are there any other questions?

Yes, Mr. DeWine.

Mr. DEWINE. Maybe I shouldn't even say this, but I'm going to anyway, I just—without getting into the merits of the testimony in this hearing today, it just strikes me that—and I wasn't here in Congress 25 or 30 years ago, but I would be willing to bet that there was a hearing very similar to this—again, without getting into the merits of it at this point—where civil rights activists were at a table and were saying that they had a moral duty to do this, and who were saying that they had a moral right to trespass. I just make that—

Mr. SCHUMER. Will the gentleman yield?

Mr. DEWINE [continuing]. Comment without getting into the merits of it, of the issue.

Mr. SCHUMER. Will the gentleman yield?

Mr. DEWINE. I'll be more than happy to yield.

Mr. SCHUMER. I respect what the gentleman is saying, and all of us, probably, at some point in our lives, have to decide—maybe at some point in our lives—probably all of us don't, but certainly some of us, at some points in our lives, have to determine when there is a higher law that we must follow. The point, though, is that Government, whether it be local government, or State government, or Federal Government, cannot, if it's going to have any legitimacy, sit idly by.

If Mr. Scheidler were to say that he is violating the law because he is following a higher moral code, as other people in this country have done, and then the local authorities or the Federal authorities were to say, "OK, Mr. Scheidler, you've done what you've done, you've made your statement, now you must serve time in jail, because your moral law is not our national law," we'd have no need for the hearing today. . . .

The issue here today, in those civil rights laws, the minute that somebody sat at a lunch counter, violating a law that they thought was morally repugnant to them, they were hauled away and they were put in jail. And they served in jail, and then they became martyrs or at least a symbol to a movement that grew. What we are saying here in this hearing today, or what we're exploring, is the fact that these acts are occurring and neither local government, state government nor federal government is doing its duty to enforce the law. That's the difference. . . .

Mr. CONYERS. Mr. Chairman, I would like to observe, in this analysis and comparison of the civil rights movement to this activity today, which I think is totally not related, that the members of the civil rights movement were not engaged in assaulting, damaging, they were not attacking the property of other people. As a matter of fact, they were nonviolently motivated.

Mr. DEWINE. Would the gentleman yield for a moment?

Mr. SCHEIDLER. Watts, Detroit, Chicago.

Mr. CONYERS. Just a moment. As a matter of fact, they were put upon and were attacked, especially in Chicago, I particularly remember. But the whole comparison between the civil rights movement and a nonviolent protest in which there were violations of State law is totally incomparable to the harassment, intimidation, bombing that is going on that was not a part of the civil rights movement. . . .

Mr. DEWINE. Just this one last comment. I know the chairman wants to finish up the meeting; I don't blame him.

The same arguments were made in the civil rights movement. They were made. The question of—the moral question, the tough moral question—do I have the right to violate a State law and trespass, those issues were brought up in the civil rights movement, too. That's all I'm saying. I'm not saying that he's right on the question of trespass. I'm not saying I would trespass in knowing violation of the law. . . .

[Whereupon, at 12:36 p.m., the subcommittee was adjourned.]

18

ANITA BRYANT

When the Homosexuals Burn the Holy Bible in Public . . . How Can I Stand By Silently

ca. 1977

Former beauty queen and recording artist Anita Bryant jumped into politics in 1977 in her adopted hometown of Miami (Dade County) to overturn a new ordinance that affirmed the rights of gays and lesbians. This newsletter explains the mission and goals of her work in the wake of the Dade County victory.

Dear Friend:
    <u>I don't hate the homosexuals!</u>
    But as a mother, I must protect my children from their evil influence. And I am sure you have heard about my fight here in Dade County, Florida—and nationwide—for the rights of my children and yours.
    <u>But I had no idea my speaking out would lead to such frightening consequences:</u>
    . . . ugly persecution at the hands of militant homosexual groups.
    . . . the attempted blacklisting of my career.
    . . . constant bitter threats to shut me up for good.
    . . . misguided individuals hounding me and my family—
        even when we go to church.
    All this, because I stood up for my children—as a mother—as an American—as a Christian.
    Then, when the militant homosexuals lost the public vote in Dade County, their friends in New England <u>burned the Holy Bible!</u>
    And now there is a group that wants to produce a motion picture that portrays Jesus Christ as a homosexual . . .*
    That's why I am writing you today—because I cannot remain silent while radical, militant homosexuals are raising millions of dollars and

---

Note: All ellipses in this document are in the original.—Ed.

Anita Bryant, "When the Homosexuals Burn the Holy Bible in Public . . . How Can I Stand By Silently" (Anita Bryant Ministries, ca. 1977).

waging a campaign for special privileges under the disguise of "civil rights"...

...and they claim they are a legitimate minority group.

Do you realize what they want?

They want to recruit our school children under the protection of the laws of our land!

Already San Francisco has a local ordinance with age of consent down to 14, and the school board has ordered homosexuality to be taught as an alternate lifestyle in all the sex education classes.

All this is why I have formed a new organization, Anita Bryant Ministries. And I am concerned about more than just one problem.

In fact, I am going to speak out against all the evil forces that threaten our children and the security of our families and all individuals.

But first, I must turn to persons like you for advice.

I must know what problems concern you.

Therefore, I am enclosing one (1) Official Public Opinion Survey Ballot for you.

Furthermore, I am requesting you to mark your ballot immediately and return it to me.

Your vote will be held in strict confidence, and my office will tabulate the opinions, so that when I write my books, give interviews and appear on nationwide television, I will be able to represent your concerns as well as my own.

For example, how do you stand on survey question number one?

(1) Do you approve of legislation allowing known practicing homosexuals to teach in public, private and religious schools?

(Yes)   (No)   (Undecided)

Please mark your ballot to indicate that you either approve, disapprove, or are undecided.

And remember, militant homosexuals want their sexual behavior and preference to be considered respectable and accepted by society.

They want to recruit your children and teach them the virtues of becoming a homosexual.

One militant homosexual group actually published a newsletter giving techniques to entice and recruit young men to commit unnatural sex acts.

And churches are even ordaining homosexual preachers! Can you imagine? Doesn't the sin of open homosexual behavior rank right along with adultery and incest?

I don't hate the homosexuals. I love them enough to tell them the truth . . .

. . . that God hates sin but He loves the sinner and He will forgive any sin if the sinner repents of his sin . . . and not flaunt it or ask the law to condone it.

And I want to help them find the love of Jesus in their own hearts and return to God's moral law.

But I insist they leave my children and your children alone. We must not give them the legal right to destroy the moral fiber of our families and our nation.

I must—and I will—protect my children.

How do you vote on this issue?

That brings me to survey question number two:

(2) Do you favor stricter laws controlling child pornography?

    (Yes)   (No)   (Undecided)

Please keep in mind that the use of young children in obscene magazines and films is growing. Even five and six year olds are being photographed and used for perverted sexual appetites.

Sometimes, for the price of an ice-cream cone, a child will pose naked for a porno film.

What a sorry state of affairs. And what a terrible attack on the values of our American life.

I believe that all sexual pictures of children must be banned by law, regardless of whether or not the pictures are "legally obscene."

And I believe that everyone who engages in this sinful profit should be arrested . . . the producer, the photographer, the printer, the distributing agent and even the salesman in the bookstore.

If the law protects the child pornographer, then the law must be changed.

As William Penn once said, "Men must be governed by God, or they'll be ruled by tyrants."

Finally, what about the problem right in your own living room?

(3) Do you favor the elimination of "R" rated movies from television and stricter controls governing sex and violence on TV?

    (Yes)   (No)   (Undecided)

That TV set in your home has the power to destroy your family. Your children are being taught to:

((... commit cold-blooded murder.
... rape, steal, get drunk, and sell drugs.
... set fire to a school building.
... run away from home.
... use vulgar language.
... become a prostitute.))

In brief, sex, violence, beatings, rape, and sexual perversion is an everyday affair and happens nightly in your living room in full view of your children.

Is the answer to smash your TV set? Perhaps. But first, let's give TV a chance. Let's try to clean it up.

You and I must share the blame with the TV producers. We have not spoken out. We have failed to stand up for our convictions.

Your children know what's going on. When an "R" rated movie is being shown, the explicit rape scene may be cut out . . .

. . . or when the axe splits the skull of a kindly old man, you don't see his brains spill out on the pavement, but your child knows what has happened.

All this is such a shame because television can be a wonderful force for good.

Will you cast your ballot on these burning issues threatening our daily lives?

I must hear from you immediately, because I cannot carry on this fight by myself.

Some liberal newspapers are saying "Anita Bryant should be shut up."

But what do you say? Shall I be silent?

And if you want me to speak out, will you consider sending a special love gift to support the work of Anita Bryant Ministries?

I am following the leadership of the Lord—and already it has cost me a great deal, but it is worth it to protect my children and yours . . .

. . . and take a stand for what is moral and right in our nation.

In fact the Bible says, "If God be for you, who can be against you?"

I believe this with all my heart and so does my husband, Bob Green, who has been with me since this fight first started . . .

. . . and now we have a peace with our Lord that surpasses all understanding, and with His guidance in our lives, we are not afraid for our lives, or for our family.

So there you have it. All I can do is turn to you. I must know how you feel on these burning issues.

And I must depend on your $10 tax deductible gift of love—or perhaps even $15 or $25 or $100, if these issues really shake you as they do me.

May I hear from you immediately?

As you know, the militant homosexuals are always preparing massive public relations campaigns . . .

. . . will you help me stop the militant homosexuals?

. . . and stop the evil child pornography business?

. . . and stop the sex and violence on television?

Please mark your official Public Opinion Survey Ballot immediately, and return it and your gift of love to me in the reply envelope I am enclosing.

And by the way, I will be reporting the results of the Ballot to you in my newsletter, "Anita Bryant Ministries."

So for now, thanks so much, and God bless you.

Much love from all of us.

Your friend,

Anita Bryant

19

JERRY FALWELL

Homosexuality: Is It an Acceptable Lifestyle?

1978

*In the late 1970s Falwell grew increasingly concerned about the gay
liberation movement. He believed that homosexuality was a major sin
that threatened to destroy the nation. This published sermon illustrates
his views.*

Our generation has a unique challenge unknown to other decades. It is
more serious than drunkenness, the spread of narcotics or the spread
of crime. It is the growing cancer of homosexuality, man with man and
woman with woman. I believe this crime is so serious it could destroy
mankind.

In my age, we laughed at queers, fairies and anyone who was thought
to be a homosexual. It was a hideous thing and no one talked about it,
much less ever confessed to being a homosexual. Now they are coming
out of the closet.

I must preach against homosexuality because the gays have attacked
my friend, Anita Bryant. They are working in every state to repeal existing laws directed against homosexuality. Also, the powerful media lobby
(movies, magazines, TV, etc.) make homosexuality appear as an alternate and an acceptable life-style for Americans.

Homosexuality is not an acceptable life-style to Christians or to
America.

These are good reasons, but the main reason I am preaching against
homosexuality is that it is contrary to the Word of God. Let's look at several passages: "Therefore shall a man leave his father and his mother,
and shall cleave unto his wife: and they shall be one flesh. And they were
both naked, the man and his wife, and were not ashamed" (Genesis 2:24,
25). This Scripture lays the pattern for the home, the family. God plans
for one woman and one man to join together for one lifetime. God did

From Jerry Falwell, *How You Can Help Clean Up America* (Lynchburg, Va.: Liberty
Publishing Company, 1978), 67, 70–72.

not create Adam and Edward; He created Adam and Eve. The home is a positive indictment against homosexuality.

The next reference to homosexuality is in Genesis 19, in which the heavenly beings visit Sodom and are given hospitality at the home of Lot. The men of the city surround the house of Lot, and we find these words: "And they called unto Lot, and said unto him, Where are the men which came in to thee this night? bring them out unto us, that we may know them" (Genesis 19:5). Most scholars have translated the verse, "Bring the men out that we may have sexual relations with them." We read further in this same chapter that God sent fire and brimstone and destroyed the city of Sodom because of such wickedness.

Next, we find God prohibits homosexuality. "Thou shalt not lie with mankind, as with womankind: it is abomination" (Leviticus 18:22). The prohibition is repeated, "If a man also lie with mankind, as he lieth with a woman, both of them have committed an abomination: they shall surely be put to death; their blood shall be upon them" (Leviticus 20:13). In the Old Testament God required a person to be put to death for homosexuality. In the New Testament God removes the ceremonial and civic judgment, but the spiritual punishment remains. God's rules for right and wrong have never changed.

The next passage dealing with homosexuality is found in Romans. "Wherefore God also gave them up to uncleanness through the lusts of their own hearts, to dishonour their own bodies between themselves: Who changed the truth of God into a lie, and worshipped and served the creature more than the Creator, who is blessed for ever. Amen. For this cause God gave them up unto vile affections: for even their women did change the natural use into that which is against nature: And likewise also the men, leaving the natural use of the woman, burned in their lust one toward another; men with men working that which is unseemly, and receiving in themselves that recompence of their error which was meet. And even as they did not like to retain God in their knowledge, God gave them over to a reprobate mind, to do those things which are not convenient" (Romans 1:24–28). God describes the actions between men as "unseemly." I might have used the word filthy or debase, but God's mind is so pure He cannot conceive an adjective to correctly describe such sin. . . .

I am against homosexuality because it is not a victimless crime—it enslaves others. The worst thing about homosexuals is that they draw others into their net. They proselyte after the worst order—they prey on children. Little children are exploited and their bodies are ravaged by human animals.

Most homosexuals claim God put a desire within them for the same sex and they blame God for their homosexuality. But homosexuality is not a matter of genes and chromosomes. Research shows that a person has the homosexual experience before he has the homosexual desire. Usually the homosexual was trapped into his first experience before twelve years of age. Therefore he is not born that way. Homosexuals are made. And if the child enjoys the sexual experience, he is on his way to becoming a practicing homosexual.

What frightens me is that homosexuals seek out young boys. A public prosecutor testified, "The younger the sex object, the more attractive he is to the homosexual."

We have read of reports in Texas and New York where homosexuals have become workers in clubs with boys and after the homosexuals have gained the confidence of the boys, they are lured into sex acts. I must be careful because there are many wonderful organizations that help boys and girls. And it is almost impossible for them to "weed out" the homosexual who wants to work in their program. If we allow the law to be softened to protect and coddle the homosexual, it will be almost impossible to keep homosexuals from working in these good clubs. And when a practicing homosexual recruits a little boy or girl, that homosexual is the worst and lowest kind of criminal. The little boy or girl can be perverted forever and end up in hell because he became hardened to the Gospel.

I am against homosexuality because it denies the divine order of the home. God performed the first marriage and set up the first home. He brought Adam and Eve together and made them one flesh.

Because homosexuality cannot procreate, it must proselyte. If one generation rejected homosexuality, it would die out. If one generation became homosexual, there would be no next generation.

Because God will judge the nation given over to homosexuality, I believe the United States will be destroyed if we permit homosexuality as an alternate lifestyle.

In the same way, God prepares a woman to be the helpmeet for a man today. Marriage is a beautiful picture of what God expects of a man and a woman.

The Scriptures teach that women are the divinely designed counterpart to men in all areas of life—social, psychological, spiritual and physical. God endorses heterosexuality and condemns homosexuality.

I am against homosexuality because it is a sterile relationship that will destroy mankind. Homosexuality is like a disease that will spread if not contained.

On June 26, 1977, on Fifth Avenue in New York, a demonstration for gay rights was held. The marchers in that demonstration formed a front, curb to curb, 28 blocks long, and included lesbian and homosexual groups from the surrounding area. It was called the longest parade for homosexual rights in New York's history. That frightens me because when they come out of the closets, they are a much larger group than we expected.

There is no way a homosexual can practice his perversion by himself. The men in Sodom demanded that Lot bring out his heavenly guests. They wanted sexual relations with them. Like a spiritual cancer, homosexuality spread until the city of Sodom was destroyed. Can we believe that God will spare the United States if homosexuality continues to spread?

20

MARABEL MORGAN

The Total Woman

1973

In response to the sexual and feminist revolutions, conservative Christian women struggled to define their marital roles in the 1970s. This best-selling advice book by evangelical Marabel Morgan (which she dedicated in part to Anita Bryant) prescribed clear ways in which a wife could simultaneously conform to biblical norms and engage in a fulfilling sex life.

I think in superlatives, so naturally I expected that my marriage to Charlie Morgan would be the world's greatest. Both of us were determined to give our best to each other, but my knowledge of what that entailed was nil. I believed in the all-American Cinderella story; marriage was ruffly curtains at the kitchen window, strawberries for breakfast, and lovin' all the time. . . .

From Marabel Morgan, *The Total Woman* (Old Tappan, N.J.: Revell, 1973), 15, 17, 19, 22–23, 26–27, 57–58, 68–70, 91–95, 183–84.

As the months passed, however, our lives became more complicated, and we gradually changed. . . .

As the years wore on, things got worse. . . .

I didn't like it one bit. . . .

Something drastic had to be done! . . . I made a decision to change the collision course I was on. . . .

The change began with my pursuit of knowledge. I bought all the marriage books I could find. I read until I felt cross-eyed at night. I took self-improvement courses. I studied books on psychology. I studied the Bible. Over and over certain principles emerged and I began to apply them to my marriage. . . .

The results of applying certain principles to my marriage were so revolutionary that I had to pass them on in the four-lesson Total Woman course, and now in this book. . . .

This book is not intended to be the ultimate authority on marriage. Far from it. I don't pretend to have an automatic, ready-to-wear answer for every marriage problem. I do believe it is possible, however, for almost any wife to have her husband absolutely adore her in just a few weeks' time. She can revive romance, reestablish communication, break down barriers, and put sizzle back into her marriage. It really is up to her. She has the power.

If, through reading and applying these principles, you become a Total Woman, with your husband more in love with you than ever before, my efforts in writing this book will have been rewarded.

Psychiatrists tell us that a man's most basic needs, outside of warm sexual love, are approval and admiration. Women need to be loved; men need to be admired. We women would do well to remember this one important difference between us and the other half. . . .

Have you ever wondered why your husband doesn't just melt when you tell him how much you love him? But try saying, "I admire you," and see what happens. If you want to free him to express his thoughts and emotions, begin by filling up his empty cup with admiration. He must be filled first, for he has nothing to give until this need is met. And when his cup runs over, guess who lives in the overflow? Why, the very one who has been filling up the cup—you!

Love your husband and hold him in reverence, it says in the Bible. That means admire him. *Reverence*, according to the dictionary, means "To respect, honor, esteem, adore, praise, enjoy, and admire." . . .

What causes most of the problems in your marriage? I find that the conflict between two separate egos is usually the culprit—your viewpoint versus his viewpoint. If they happen to be the same, fine. If not, as so often is the case, conflict results. . . .

The biblical remedy for marital conflict is stated, "You wives must submit to your husbands' leadership in the same way you submit to the Lord.". . . God planned for woman to be under her husband's rule.

Now before you scream and throw this book away, hear me out. First of all, no one says you have to get married. If you do not wish to adapt to a man, the negative implication is to stay single. If you are married but not adapting, you probably already know that marriage isn't the glorious experience you anticipated.

Secondly, you may think, "That's not fair. I have my rights. Why shouldn't he adapt to my way first, and then maybe I'll consider doing something to please him?" I have seen many couples try this new arrangement, unsuccessfully. Unless the wife adapts to his way of life, there's no way to avoid the conflict that is certain to occur.

Thirdly, please note that I did not say a woman is inferior to man, or even that a woman should be subservient to all men, but that a wife should be under her own husband's leadership.

Fourthly, another little phrase may cause some consternation: ". . . in the same way you submit to the Lord." Perhaps you are thinking, "I don't submit to the Lord. I don't even know Him. How archaic can you get? Even if you believe in Him, who submits to Him?"

The fact is that God originally ordained marriage. He gave certain ground rules and if they are applied, a marriage will work. Otherwise, the marriage cannot be closely knit because of the inherent conflict between your husband's will and yours. The evidence is all too clearly visible. In some cities there are now more people getting divorced each day than getting married.

Man and woman, although equal in status, are different in function. God ordained man to be the head of the family, its president, and his wife to be the executive vice-president. Every organization has a leader and the family unit is no exception. There is no way you can alter or improve this arrangement. On occasion, families have tried to reverse this and have elected a woman as president. When this order is turned around, the family is upside down. The system usually breaks down within a short period of time. Allowing your husband to be your family president is just good business. . . .

Let's begin by going back to that moment when you first saw the man who is now your husband. Specifically, let's consider the first time he saw *you*. Remember how immaculate you were each time he came to call? Remember those long baths and then the powder, perfume, and pizazz? You felt so confident, and you were so excited you could hardly wait to see him. Dazzling, you floated out to meet him, knowing he would be pleased just seeing you and being seen with you.

Well, what did you look like last night when he came home? What did you have on this morning when he left for work? Girls, is it any wonder the honeymoon is over, and instead of feeling sought, you both feel caught?

It doesn't have to be that way. . . .

One of your husband's most basic needs is for you to be physically attractive to him. He loves your body; in fact, he literally craves it. The outer shell of yours is what the real estate people call "curb appeal"— how the house looks from the outside. Is your curb appeal this week what it was five years ago?

Many a husband rushes off to work leaving his wife slumped over a cup of coffee in her grubby undies. His once sexy bride is now wrapped in rollers and smells like bacon and eggs. All day long he's surrounded at the office by dazzling secretaries who emit clouds of perfume.

This is all your husband asks from you. He wants the girl of his dreams to be feminine, soft, and touchable when he comes home. That's his need. If you are dumpy, stringy, or exhausted, he's sorry he came. That first look tells him your nerves are shot, his dinner is probably shot, and you'd both like to shoot the kids. It's a bad scene. Is it any wonder so many men come home late, if at all? . . .

Take a few extra moments for that bubble bath tonight. If your husband comes home at 6:00, bathe at 5:00. . . . In preparing for your six o'clock date, lie back and let go of the tensions of the day. Think about that special man who's on his way home to you.

Remove all prickly hairs and be squeaky clean from head to toe. Be touchable and kissable. For a really sparkling mouth, use dental floss after brushing your teeth, then brush again, and close with a good mouthwash. You could greet anyone after that! . . .

Have you ever met your husband at the front door in some outrageously sexy outfit? I can hear you howl, "She's got to be kidding. My husband's not the type, and besides, we've been married twenty-one years!"

Nope, I'm not kidding, *especially* if you've been married twenty-one years. Most women dress to please other women rather than their own husbands. Your husband needs you to fulfill his daydreams. . . .

You can be lots of different women to him. Costumes provide variety without him ever leaving home. I believe that every man needs excitement and high adventure at home. Never let him know what to expect when he opens the front door; make it like opening a surprise package. You may be a smoldering sexpot, or an all-American fresh beauty. Be a pixie or a pirate—a cowgirl or a show girl. Keep him off guard. . . .

It is impossible to explain Total Woman in a ten-minute conversation, or in a four-week course, or in a how-to-do-it book. Total Woman is a way of life, a new attitude about yourself, your husband, and your children.

Total Woman starts with the premise that every woman can be made whole. Even with the complex facets to her personality and the many roles to play, no woman need go through life fragmented.

A Total Woman is not just a good housekeeper; she is a warm, loving homemaker. She is not merely a submissive sex partner; she is a sizzling lover. She is not just a nanny to her children; she is a woman who inspires them to reach out and up.

A Total Woman is a person in her own right. She has a sense of personal security and self-respect. She is not afraid to be herself. Others may challenge her standards, but she knows who she is and where she is going.

She has the gift of discovering what is worthwhile in another person. She dares her husband to rise higher than he ever dreamed. She makes marriage enjoyable instead of an endurance contest. She has a natural love affair with life and brings life to others.

You can be that Total Woman, with your priorities in order and your responsibilities in perspective. First of all, remember that you are a *person* responsible to God, your power Source. Until you become the kind of woman He wants you to be, you will not be able to fully give yourself to others, for you have little to give. Fill your cup vertically before you attempt to give to others horizontally.

Your second priority is to your husband, your *partner*. Too many husbands get lost in the shuffle after Junior arrives, or are replaced by their wives' other activities. Your husband needs to know he's tops on your list.

Your next priority is as a *parent* to your children. Good mothers are not born; they are made by women who want to be good mothers. In those early years, your children need their mom at home. Their future development is far more important than your sorority ball.

Only after you have met your spiritual needs, the needs of your husband and your children, should you think of your *profession* or the *public*. Civic clubs, parties, and social projects, yes, but only after order is restored at home.

I wish you well.
Marabel

21

Interview with Phyllis Schlafly on the Equal Rights Amendment

November 1978

Roman Catholic Phyllis Schlafly was one of the most influential conservative political activists of the twentieth century. In spite of her own very public role, Schlafly promoted traditional ideas about women and gender that resonated with millions of Americans. When in 1972 Congress passed an Equal Rights Amendment to the Constitution, which looked like it would easily be ratified by the states, Schlafly raised an army of grassroots activists to challenge it. Her work helped foster alliances between Catholics and evangelicals on family issues. The following is an interview with Schlafly conducted by conservative Christian magazine editor Gary Wall (GW).

GW: Why are you against the ERA?

PS: Because of its effect on the family. It will drive the wife out of the home, and it will take away the legal rights of wives and mothers.

My major objections can be stated in three parts. First it is a fraud. It doesn't do anything for women. It doesn't give them any rights, opportunities, or benefits that they don't have now. Most of the real objectives have been covered by existing legislation—The Equal Employment Opportunity Act of 1972, the education amendments of 1972, and the Equal Credit Opportunity Act of 1974.

Second, Section One of the ERA is designed to convert us into a unisex society. It would prevent us from making any distinction between men and woman. So the next time we have a war, women would have to be drafted and put in combat just like men. You couldn't have laws that say a husband must support his wife. You couldn't give any preferential treatment to wives, mothers, and widows. You wouldn't be able to make a reasonable, common sense separation of treatment such as

"Dialogue with Phyllis Schlafly," *Moody Monthly*, November 1978, 44–49.

in single sex schools, fraternities, or athletics; or in other areas such as prison regulations and insurance regulations.

ERA also makes it impossible to have any laws against homosexuals. They would have to be treated with the same rights as husbands and wives because you couldn't discriminate on the basis of sex.

Third, ERA would shift most of the remaining powers of the states to Washington, including power over marriage, divorce, child custody, prison regulations, insurance rates, homosexual laws—any type of legislation that has traditionally distinguished between men and women.

GW: Do you see any good things in the ERA?

PS: Nothing, because I see it as anti-family. If it is anti-family, nothing can be good about it. It is the vehicle for achievement for certain radical, political, and social goals. . . .

GW: Why are you against women's liberation?

PS: I used to think I was against it because there was more bad than is good about it. But after working with these people, I know there is nothing good about it. Women's lib is anti-family, and once you realize that, nothing is good about it. Women's lib is a major cause of divorce. What it does to a woman is much like a disease. It is particularly contagious among women in their forties, especially after the children go off to school. Libbers tell these women, "You poor creature. You've wasted your life. You don't have an identity of your own. Go and seek your own self-fulfillment under your own name."

Women in that age group are walking out on marriages in tremendous numbers. These breakups don't have the typical causes—adultery, alcohol, and money.

Besides the bitter women who are ripe for anyone to tell them how mistreated they've been—this is the basic leadership constituency—are the young college educated women and college girls. They've had some women's study courses and have been told that the worst career in the world is homemaking.

Women's lib is basically a negative approach toward life. They tell women, "The cards are stacked against you. If you get a job, you won't get promoted and will never be treated fairly. If you get married life is nothing but a bunch of dirty diapers and dishes because your husband will treat you like a servant." After they flatten them with this negativism, they say, "Seek self-fulfillment over every other value."

There's no percentage in marrying a girl who isn't willing to take care of her children. If they want to set their values that way, nobody's stopping them. But it isn't compatible with a happy marriage and motherhood.

GW: In their literature, the radical feminists say they want to do away with family, love, marriage, heterosex, and religion. Can they accomplish that with the ERA?

PS: Yes. It is the vehicle to achieve all their goals. If the wife's support is taken away—as I believe ERA will do, she will need to get a job. When that happens, you take away the child's right to have his mother in the house. The next step is what the Ohio task force on the ERA proposes: child care centers for all children. This puts children in an institution. Legalized abortion is a main goal of the woman's movement because they look upon women's susceptibility to pregnancy as a grave injustice.

In seeking their total independence from men, women want to make homosexuals entitled to the same dignity and respect husbands and wives have. ERA is the vehicle that would enable them to achieve this. ERA says you can't deny or abridge any right on account of sex. So how can you deny a marriage license under ERA to two men or two women? Can they do it? They get their people in the government and work for it with our money.

GW: How have the radical feminists done this?

PS: They started with nothing. But they have worked hard. . . .

The feminists are making our laws. They are taking over our educational system and the media and they are going to get all the male jobs, too. This is their goal. . . .

GW: What are your other problems with feminists?

PS: They are in league with pornographers. Two of the biggest and best known adult men's magazines give them money. They are a powerful anti-family force. You don't see any pictures of families with children in these magazines. . . .

I consider pornography the ultimate degradation of women. It's an anti-family movement.

GW: You say the feminists want to change male and female roles, but what about the women who are happy in their role and don't want to work outside the home?

PS: They can get to her. I have friends whose husbands have been told they won't get a promotion for ten years because all the promotions are going to women to bring up their quotas. Then she will find it hard to live on one income.

Another plan feminists have is to change Social Security so that the husband has to pay a tax on the assumed earnings of his wife. This would cost an additional $1,000 a year in federal tax for the privilege of having the wife in the home. . . .

GW: What is the link between feminist and ERA forces and the lesbian groups?

PS: The National Women's Conference in Houston is where they joined together. Prior to Houston, women's lib had not been able to define their relationship. But there, they were all in the same conference, on the same commission, with identifiable names and goals, and they passed their resolutions. They got the whole group to close ranks on everything, including the privileges for homosexuals to teach and have child custody and so forth.

They got all the libbers who prior to that time had not been pro-lesbian to join ranks. Betty Friedan is a good example. For the first time, she said that they had to work together. The National Organization for Women (NOW) has always been for the lesbian.

5

God and the GOP

22

PAT ROBERTSON

Action Plan for the 1980s
1979

In 1979 religious broadcaster and cable television pioneer Pat Robertson laid out an action plan for the 1980s. The plan represented the core ideas fueling the rise of the Religious Right. Nine years later Robertson mounted his own campaign for the presidency based on the principles outlined here. Although he did not win the Republican nomination, his actions in 1988 helped lay the foundation for the Christian Coalition and the continuing success of the Religious Right.

October, 1979 marks the 50th anniversary of the Great Depression of 1929—an event which did more to shape the existing framework of U.S. government policy than any other single event in recent history. Out of the Depression came a powerful central government; an imperial presidency; the enormous political power of newspapers, radio, and later television; an anti-business bias in the country; powerful unions; a complexity of federal regulations and agencies designed to control and, in many instances, protect powerful vested interests; and, more importantly, the belief in the economic policy of British scholar John Maynard

Records of National Religious Broadcasters, file 6, box 29, collection 309, Billy Graham Center Archives, Wheaton, Ill.

Keynes, to the end that government spending and government "fine tuning" would guarantee perpetual prosperity.

New Deal Keynesian policies did reverse the economic tragedy of the Depression (with the help of World War II). But many now feel that the "cure" of the '30s is the cause of the sickness of the '70s. In fact, many knowledgeable observers are contending that forces unleashed in the post-Depression days have so weakened Western civilization, and the United States in particular, that a radical change is on the way. Some feel that 1979 may be the watershed year for the Western nations as we now know them. . . .

Six Steps to Moral, Political, and Economic Recovery

As 1979 draws to a close, we are left with a 50-year legacy which should cause alarm. Our domestic strength has been weakened by government excesses and mismanagement; our capacity for national sacrifice and resolute action may have been reduced to a level of ineffectiveness; vital raw materials necessary to our economic and military survival are in the hands of others; and we are confronted by a powerful adversary with both the capability and the desire to destroy us.

We urgently need two things. First, that God will hold our external enemies at bay while confusing their counsels against us. Second, we need a bold, dynamic plan based on practical reality which will permit our nation to turn around and begin the slow road to moral, political, and economic recovery.

A national strategy for the 80s must be formulated. Each individual needs a similar personal plan. Here are some suggestions intended to stimulate thought.

(1) There must be a profound moral revival in the land.

Not only increased evangelism; not a glib confession of faith, but a profound commitment to Jesus Christ and biblical Christianity. There must be true repentance, fasting, prayer, and calling upon God. The "people who are called by His name" need to beseech God with all humility on behalf of our nation and our world. A miracle is needed and we must ask for one.

(2) Those who love God must get involved in the election of strong leaders.

Men and women of good will across the land must join together to ensure the election of strong leaders who are beholden to no special interest group; who are pledged to reduce the size of government, eliminate federal deficits, free our productive capacity, ensure sound currency; who are pledged to strong national defense, and do not confuse peace with surrender; who recognize the anti-Christ nature of Marxism and will refuse to permit innocent people to fall victim to Marxist tyranny; who support programs which encourage godliness while resisting programs which result in the triumph of humanism and atheism in our land.

More than anything we need leaders who are not afraid to demand necessary sacrifices of our people in order to free us from bondage — whether it comes from the OPEC cartel, from crushing debt, from nuclear blackmail, or from the poverty and helplessness of a portion of our people.

To accomplish this takes work. Christians must register to vote, work within parties, attend caucuses, mass meetings, and conventions. They need to be informed on issues and know what each candidate stands for. They must be willing to hold public office and, where appropriate, should prepare for government service. They must be willing to write letters, make telephone calls, lobby for legislation, and pray for their leaders. In short, they must be good citizens. In the Book of Proverbs we read, "The diligent will bear rule, but the slothful will be put to forced labor." If Christians want to rule, they must be diligent. There is no magic shortcut.

(3) In a moral sense, we must recognize our right to preserve our precious religious heritage.

Supreme Court decisions are not holy writ. The damage to our spiritual and moral heritage that has been brought on by the Supreme Court school prayer decisions is beyond calculation. President Roosevelt did not hesitate to use power to force the Supreme Court to acquiesce to New Deal legislation. Christians should not hesitate to use the lawful power at their disposal to secure reversal of onerous Supreme Court decisions.

(4) Christians must take action in education.

The courts and ill-advised federal regulations have often made a mockery of education. Eliminating prayer removed moral restraints; busing tends to remove neighborhood restraints. Many schools have become undisciplined jungles.

Textbooks used in public schools often tend to destroy long-established moral values. Parents have every right to insist on quality moral education for their children. They should fight for it in public schools, and if good public education is denied them, they must do everything possible to establish an alternative private system of education where Christian values can be taught.

(5) Christians must become aware of the awesome power of the media to mold our moral and political consensus.

Christians need to do everything in their power to get involved in media (radio, television, newspapers, magazines). Where possible, Christians should seek to establish or purchase newspapers, magazines, radio stations, and television stations.

Christians should learn motion picture techniques, produce drama, write music, publish books—anything to produce a climate of righteousness and godliness. They must dispel the sense of nihilism and lack of meaning that is so evident in much that passes for art these days.

(6) Christians should seek positions of leadership in major corporations and benevolent foundations.

It has been said that money is the "mother's milk" of politics. It also is the essential nourishment of education, entrance into media, the arts, and wide-scale evangelism. Christians should learn the ways of finance: stocks, bonds, banking, commodities, real estate, taxes. More than anything, they should learn and apply the principles of God's kingdom dealing with the acquisition and use of wealth. When they have accumulated material resources, they should recognize the enormous good they can accomplish with that wealth in unity with other members of the body of Christ throughout the world.

The Keys to Success: Faith and Diligence

The Communists, who espouse a false religion, after only 60 years dominate the world. The reason is simple—they were dedicated to their cause and they worked at it. Except for our Lord's return, we cannot expect our nation or our world to be freed from tyranny in one year or even 10 years. But if we are faithful and diligent, with His blessing, it will be done.

"The kingdoms of this world are become the kingdoms of our Lord, and of His Christ; and He shall reign for ever and ever."
(Rev. 11:15)

23

JERRY FALWELL

Organizing the Moral Majority
1980

In 1980 Falwell laid out his argument for Christian political activism, setting much of the 1980s political agenda for conservative Christians. By this point Falwell had emerged as the best-known spokesperson for the burgeoning Religious Right.

In light of our present moral condition, we as a nation are quickly approaching the point of no return. There can be no doubt that the sin of America is severe. We are literally approaching the brink of national disaster. Many have exclaimed, "If God does not judge America soon, He will have to apologize to Sodom and Gomorrah." In almost every aspect of our society, we have flaunted our sinful behavior in the very face of God Himself. Our movies, television programs, magazines, and entertainment in general are morally bankrupt and spiritually corrupt. We have become one of the most blatantly sinful nations of all time. We dare not continue to excuse ourselves on the basis of God's past blessing in our national heritage. The time for a national repentance of God's people has now come to America. . . .

Is there no hope? Is our doom inevitable? Can the hand of God's judgment not be stayed? Many of us are convinced that it can. We believe that there is yet an opportunity for a reprieve in God's judgment of this great nation. But that hope rests in the sincerity of national repentance led by the people of God. . . .

While sins of America are certainly many, let us summarize the five major problems that have political consequences, political implications, that moral Americans need to be ready to face.

1. ABORTION—Nine men, by majority vote, said it was okay to kill unborn children. In 1973, two hundred million Americans and four hundred thousand pastors stood by and did little to

---

From Jerry Falwell, *Listen, America!* (Garden City, N.Y.: Doubleday, 1980), 217, 219, 221, 223, 225–34.

stop it. Every year millions of babies are murdered in America, and most of us want to forget that it is happening. The Nazis murdered six million Jews, and certainly the Nazis fell under the hand of the judgment of God for these atrocities. So-called Christian America has murdered more unborn innocents than that. How do we think that we shall escape the judgment of God?

2. HOMOSEXUALITY—In spite of the fact that the Bible clearly designates this sin as an act of a "reprobate mind" for which God "gave them up" (Rm. 1:26–28), our government seems determined to legalize homosexuals as a legitimate "minority." . . . Even the ancient Greeks, among whom homosexuality was fairly prevalent, never legally condoned its practice. Plato himself called it "abnormal." If our nation legally recognizes homosexuality, we will put ourselves under the same hand of judgment as Sodom and Gomorrah.

3. PORNOGRAPHY—The four-billion-dollar-per-year pornographic industry is probably the most devastating moral influence of all upon our young people. Sex magazines deliberately increase the problem of immoral lust and thus provoke increased adultery, prostitution, and sexual child abuse. . . .

4. HUMANISM—The contemporary philosophy that glorifies man as man, apart from God, is the ultimate outgrowth of evolutionary science and secular education. In his new book *The Battle for the Mind,* Dr. Tim LaHaye argues that the full admission of humanism as the religion of secular education came after prayer and Bible reading were excluded from our public schools. Ultimately, humanism rests upon the philosophy of existentialism, which emphasizes that one's present existence is the true meaning and purpose of life. Existentialism has become the religion of the public schools. Applied to psychology, it postulates a kind of moral neutrality that is detrimental to Christian ethics. In popular terminology it explains, "Do your own thing," and "If it feels good, do it!" It is an approach to life that has no room for God and makes man the measure of all things.

5. THE FRACTURED FAMILY—With a skyrocketing divorce rate, the American family may well be on the verge of extinction in the next twenty years. Even the recent White House

Conference on Families has called for an emphasis on diverse family forums (common-law, communal, homosexual, and transsexual "marriages"). The Bible pattern of the family has been virtually discarded by modern American society. Our movies and magazines have glorified the physical and emotional experience of sex without love to the point that most Americans do not even consider love to be important at all anymore. Bent on self-gratification, we have reinterpreted our moral values in light of our immoral life styles. Since the family is the basic unit of society, and since the family is desperately in trouble today, we can conclude that our society itself is in danger of total collapse. We are not moving toward an alternate family life style, we are moving closer to the brink of destruction. . . .

Moral Americans can make the difference in America if we are willing to exert the effort to make our feelings known and if we are willing to make the necessary sacrifices to get the job done. . . .

To change America we must be involved, and this includes three areas of political action:

1. *REGISTRATION*

    A recent national poll indicated that eight million American evangelicals are not registered to vote. I am convinced that this is one of the major sins of the church today. Until concerned Christian citizens become registered voters there is very little that we can do to change the tide of political influence on the social issues in our nation. Those who object to Christians being involved in the political process are ultimately objecting to Christians being involved in the social process. The political process is really nothing more than a realization of the social process. For us to divorce ourselves from society would be to run into the kind of isolationism and monasticism that characterized the medieval hermits. Many Christians are not even aware of the importance of registering to vote. It is perfectly legal, for example, for a deputy registrar to come right to your local church at a designated time and register the entire congregation. I am convinced that those of us who are pastors have an obligation to urge our people to register to vote. I am more concerned that people exercise their freedom to vote than I am concerned for whom they vote.

2. *INFORMATION*

Many moral Americans are unaware of the real issues affecting them today. Many people do not know the voting record of their congressman and have no idea how he is representing them on political issues that have moral implications. This is one of the major reasons why we have established the Moral Majority organization. We want to keep the public informed on the vital moral issues. The Moral Majority, Inc., is a nonprofit organization, with headquarters in Washington, D.C. Our goal is to exert a significant influence on the spiritual and moral direction of our nation by: (a) mobilizing the grassroots of moral Americans in one clear and effective voice; (b) informing the moral majority what is going on behind their backs in Washington and in state legislatures across the country; (c) lobbying intensely in Congress to defeat left-wing, social-welfare bills that will further erode our precious freedom; (d) pushing for positive legislation such as that to establish the Family Protection Agency, which will ensure a strong, enduring America; and (e) helping the moral majority in local communities to fight pornography, homosexuality, the advocacy of immorality in school textbooks, and other issues facing each and every one of us.

Christians must keep America great by being willing to go into the halls of Congress, by getting laws passed that will protect the freedom and liberty of her citizens. The Moral Majority, Inc., was formed to acquaint Americans everywhere with the tragic decline in our nation's morals and to provide leadership in establishing an effective coalition of morally active citizens who are (a) prolife, (b) profamily, (c) promoral, and (d) pro-American. If the vast majority of Americans (84 per cent, according to George Gallup) still believe the Ten Commandments are valid today, why are we permitting a few leading amoral humanists and naturalists to take over the most influential positions in this nation?

Tim LaHaye has formed a code of minimum moral standards dictated by the Bible; his code would be used to evaluate the stand of candidates on moral issues. These minimum standards are:

> a. Do you agree that this country was founded on a belief in God and the moral principles of the Bible? Do you concur

that this country has been departing from those principles and needs to return to them?

b. Would you favor stricter laws relating to the sale of pornography?

c. Do you favor stronger laws against the use and sale of hard drugs?

d. Are you in favor of legalizing marijuana?

e. Would you favor legalizing prostitution?

f. Do you approve of abortions on demand when the life of the mother is not in danger?

g. Do you favor laws that would increase homosexual rights?

h. Would you vote to prevent known homosexuals to teach in schools?

i. Do you favor capital punishment for capital offenses?

j. Do you favor the right of parents to send their children to private schools?

k. Do you favor voluntary prayer in the public schools?

l. Do you favor removal of the tax-exempt status of churches?

m. Do you favor removal of the tax-exempt status of church-related schools?

n. Do you believe that government should remove children from their parents' home except in cases of physical abuse?

o. Do you favor sex education, contraceptives, or abortions for minors without parental consent?

p. Except in wartime or dire emergency, would you vote for government spending that exceeds revenue?

q. Do you favor a reduction in taxes to allow families more spendable income?

r. Do you favor a reduction in government?

s. Do you favor passage of the Equal Rights Amendment?

t. Do you favor busing schoolchildren out of their neighborhood to achieve racial integration?

u. Do you favor more federal involvement in education?

The answers to these questions would be evaluated in the light of scriptural principles. . . .

3. MOBILIZATION

The history of the church includes the history of Christian involvement in social issues. . . .

Since government has the power to control various areas and activities of our lives, it is vital that we as concerned Americans understand the importance of our involvement in the political process. . . .

America was born in her churches, and she must be reborn there as well. The time has come for pastors and church leaders to clearly and boldly proclaim the Gospel of regeneration in Christ Jesus. We need a return to God and to the Bible as never before in the history of America. Undoubtedly we are at the edge of eternity. Some are already referring to us as "post-Christian America." We have stretched the rubber band of morality too far already. A few more stretches and it will undoubtedly snap forever. When that happens we will become like all the other nations preceding us who've fallen under the judgment of God. I love America not because of her pride, her wealth, or her prestige; I love America because she, above all the nations of the world, has honored the principles of the Bible. America has been great because she has been good. . . .

I am convinced that we need a spiritual and moral revival in America if America is to survive the twentieth century. The time for action is now; we dare not wait for someone else to take up the banner of righteousness in our generation. We have already waited too long. . . .

Right living must be re-established as an American way of life. We as American citizens must recommit ourselves to the faith of our fathers and to the premises and moral foundations upon which this country was established. Now is the time to begin calling America back to God, back to the Bible, back to morality! We must be willing to live by the moral convictions that we claim to believe. There is no way that we will ever be willing to die for something for which we are not willing to live. The authority of Bible morality must once again be recognized as the legitimate guiding principle of our nation. Our love for our fellow man must ever be grounded in the truth and never be allowed to blind us from the truth that is the basis of our love for our fellow man.

As a pastor and as a parent I am calling my fellow American citizens to unite in a moral crusade for righteousness in our generation. It is time to call America back to her moral roots. It is time to call America back to God. We need a revival of righteous living based on a proper confession of sin and repentance of heart if we are to remain the land of the free and the home of the brave! I am convinced that God is calling millions of Americans in the so-often silent majority to join in the moral-majority crusade to turn America around in our lifetime. Won't you begin now to pray with us for revival in America? Let us unite our hearts and lives together for the cause of a new America . . . a moral America in which righteousness will exalt this nation. Only as we do this can we exempt ourselves from one day having to look our children in the eyes and answer this searching question: "Mom and Dad, where were you the day freedom died in America?"

The choice is now ours.

24

Evangelicals Share Their Concerns with President Jimmy Carter

January 21, 1980

By early 1980 President Jimmy Carter realized that the religious vote was becoming increasingly important. He invited the nation's most influential and media-savvy evangelical leaders to the White House for a discussion over breakfast. Each person was allowed to ask the president one question. The questions, submitted in advance, are listed in this document. They illustrate the issues that were most important to evangelicals on the eve of the pivotal 1980 presidential campaign.

1. James Kennedy, Pastor of Coral Ridge Presbyterian Church, Fort Lauderdale, Fla.

> Question: Mr. President, we are worried about our state of military preparedness. From many retired generals and admirals we have heard how terribly vulnerable the United States is to Soviet attack both in terms of military capability and civil defence. Would you tell us about our national defence capability. Would you also

Bob Maddox, Memo: Questions for the President at the Breakfast, January 21, 1980, National Religious Broadcasters Breakfast folder, box 107, Public Outreach Files, Robert Maddox Papers, Jimmy Carter Presidential Library, Atlanta, Ga.

address yourself to your personal and our national will to strike if necessary? . . .

2. Dr. Tim LaHaye, Pastor and national leader of family life conferences.
Question: Mr. President, while we know of your personal commitment to the family, we are deeply concerned about the strength of the American family. Unfortunately we feel that the government often seems to undercut the family through federal policies. Our immediate concern is the White House Conference on the Family. There are reports that the conference seems to be leaning toward a weak, liberal interpretation of the family. What can you do to facilitate government's support of the family, or at least to keep the government from undercutting the family? . . .

3. Dr. Jerry Falwell, pastor and national TV minister.
Mr. President, we would like for you [to] tell us again your stand on abortion. We are especially concerned about federal money being funnelled off into pro-abortion activities. . . .

4. Jim Bakker, President PTL Christian Network.
It seems to many of us that government agencies like the Federal Communications Commission and the Internal Revenue Service continue to interject themselves into churches and other institutions of religion. We do not expect preferential treatment and we are deeply commited to obeying the law, not only in its letter but its spirit. However, we do often get the idea when dealing with government regulatory agencies that persons on those agencies are out to "get" religious broadcasters and Christian schools. How do you respond to that problem? . . .

5. Robert Dugan, Washington representative of National Association of Evangelicals.
Question: According to a recent poll, 75% of the American public would like to see the possibility of voluntary prayer restored to the public schools. How do you feel about prayer in public schools and how do you react to legislation that seeks to permit the states to decide for themselves about prayer in public schools? . . .

6. Morris Sheats, Pastor of Beverly Hills Baptist Church, Dallas, Texas.
Question: Mr. President, with conservative evangelical Christians increasing in numbers, and knowing of your own deep personal faith,

many of us wonder why you have not placed an identifiably evangelical Christian either on your senior staff or in the cabinet? . . .

7. Oral Roberts, TV Preacher.
Mr. President, many of us feel a deep yearning for a moral and spiritual awakening in our country. We feel that you have the same desire.
Would you tell us how you feel about the spiritual and moral climate
in the country and what you as President can do to strengthen the
national character?

25

RONALD REAGAN

Remarks at the Annual Convention of the National Association of Evangelicals

March 8, 1983

*Although Ronald Reagan was not an active evangelical, he understood
the power of conservative Christians and worked to channel their energy
toward the achievement of his goals. In this address before the National
Association of Evangelicals two years after becoming president, he identified the ways in which he supported the agenda of the Religious Right and
linked faith to his cold war foreign policy.*

Well, I'm pleased to be here today with you who are keeping America
great by keeping her good. Only through your work and prayers and
those of millions of others can we hope to survive this perilous century
and keep alive this experiment in liberty, this last, best hope of man.

I want you to know that this administration is motivated by a political philosophy that sees the greatness of America in you, her people,
and in your families, churches, neighborhoods, communities—the

Ronald Reagan, "Remarks at the Annual Convention of the National Association of
Evangelicals," March 8, 1983, www.presidency.ucsb.edu/ws/index.php?pid=41023&st=
NATIONAL+ASSOCIATION+OF+EVANGELICALS&st1=#ixzz1KHxyOkc0.

institutions that foster and nourish values like concern for others and respect for the rule of law under God.

Now, I don't have to tell you that this puts us in opposition to, or at least out of step with, a prevailing attitude of many who have turned to a modern-day secularism, discarding the tried and time-tested values upon which our very civilization is based. No matter how well intentioned, their value system is radically different from that of most Americans. And while they proclaim that they're freeing us from superstitions of the past, they've taken upon themselves the job of superintending us by government rule and regulation. Sometimes their voices are louder than ours, but they are not yet a majority. . . .

Freedom prospers when religion is vibrant and the rule of law under God is acknowledged. When our Founding Fathers passed the first amendment, they sought to protect churches from government interference. They never intended to construct a wall of hostility between government and the concept of religious belief itself.

The evidence of this permeates our history and our government. The Declaration of Independence mentions the Supreme Being no less than four times. "In God We Trust" is engraved on our coinage. The Supreme Court opens its proceedings with a religious invocation. And the Members of Congress open their sessions with a prayer. I just happen to believe the schoolchildren of the United States are entitled to the same privileges as Supreme Court Justices and Congressmen.

Last year, I sent the Congress a constitutional amendment to restore prayer to public schools. Already this session, there's growing bipartisan support for the amendment, and I am calling on the Congress to act speedily to pass it and to let our children pray. . . .

Senators Denton and Hatfield have proposed legislation in the Congress on the whole question of prohibiting discrimination against religious forms of student speech. Such legislation could go far to restore freedom of religious speech for public school students. And I hope the Congress considers these bills quickly. And with your help, I think it's possible we could also get the constitutional amendment through the Congress this year.

More than a decade ago, a Supreme Court decision literally wiped off the books of 50 States statutes protecting the rights of unborn children. Abortion on demand now takes the lives of up to 15 million unborn children a year. Human life legislation ending this tragedy will some day pass the Congress, and you and I must never rest until it does. Unless and until it can be proven that the unborn child is not a living entity, then its right to life, liberty, and the pursuit of happiness must be protected. . . .

You may remember that when abortion on demand began, many, and, indeed, I'm sure many of you, warned that the practice would lead to a decline in respect for human life, that the philosophical premises used to justify abortion on demand would ultimately be used to justify other attacks on the sacredness of human life—infanticide or mercy killing. Tragically enough, those warnings proved all too true. . . .

Recent legislation introduced in the Congress by Representative Henry Hyde of Illinois not only increases restrictions on publicly financed abortions, it also addresses this whole problem of infanticide. I urge the Congress to begin hearings and to adopt legislation that will protect the right of life to all children, including the disabled or handicapped.

Now, I'm sure that you must get discouraged at times, but you've done better than you know, perhaps. There's a great spiritual awakening in America, a renewal of the traditional values that have been the bedrock of America's goodness and greatness.

One recent survey by a Washington-based research council concluded that Americans were far more religious than the people of other nations; 95 percent of those surveyed expressed a belief in God and a huge majority believed the Ten Commandments had real meaning in their lives. And another study has found that an overwhelming majority of Americans disapprove of adultery, teenage sex, pornography, abortion, and hard drugs. And this same study showed a deep reverence for the importance of family ties and religious belief.

I think the items that we've discussed here today must be a key part of the Nation's political agenda. For the first time the Congress is openly and seriously debating and dealing with the prayer and abortion issues—and that's enormous progress right there. I repeat: America is in the midst of a spiritual awakening and a moral renewal. And with your Biblical keynote, I say today, "Yes, let justice roll on like a river, righteousness like a never-failing stream."

Now, obviously, much of this new political and social consensus I've talked about is based on a positive view of American history, one that takes pride in our country's accomplishments and record. But we must never forget that no government schemes are going to perfect man. We know that living in this world means dealing with what philosophers would call the phenomenology of evil or, as theologians would put it, the doctrine of sin.

There is sin and evil in the world, and we're enjoined by Scripture and the Lord Jesus to oppose it with all our might. Our nation, too, has a legacy of evil with which it must deal. The glory of this land has been its capacity for transcending the moral evils of our past. For example, the long struggle of minority citizens for equal rights, once a source of disunity and civil war, is now a point of pride for all Americans. We must never go back. There is no room for racism, anti-Semitism, or other forms of ethnic and racial hatred in this country. . . .

But whatever sad episodes exist in our past, any objective observer must hold a positive view of American history, a history that has been the story of hopes fulfilled and dreams made into reality. Especially in this century, America has kept alight the torch of freedom, but not just for ourselves but for millions of others around the world.

And this brings me to my final point today. During my first press conference as President, in answer to a direct question, I pointed out that, as good Marxist-Leninists, the Soviet leaders have openly and publicly declared that the only morality they recognize is that which will further their cause, which is world revolution. I think I should point out I was only quoting Lenin, their guiding spirit, who said in 1920 that they repudiate all morality that proceeds from supernatural ideas—that's their name for religion—or ideas that are outside class conceptions. Morality is entirely subordinate to the interests of class war. And everything is moral that is necessary for the annihilation of the old, exploiting social order and for uniting the proletariat.

Well, I think the refusal of many influential people to accept this elementary fact of Soviet doctrine illustrates an historical reluctance to see totalitarian powers for what they are. We saw this phenomenon in the 1930's. We see it too often today.

This doesn't mean we should isolate ourselves and refuse to seek an understanding with them. I intend to do everything I can to persuade them of our peaceful intent, to remind them that it was the West that refused to use its nuclear monopoly in the forties and fifties for territorial gain and which now proposes [a] 50-percent cut in strategic ballistic missiles and the elimination of an entire class of land-based, intermediate-range nuclear missiles.

At the same time, however, they must be made to understand we will never compromise our principles and standards. We will never give away our freedom. We will never abandon our belief in God. And we will never stop searching for a genuine peace. But we can assure none of these things America stands for through the so-called nuclear freeze solutions proposed by some. . . .

A number of years ago, I heard a young father,[1] a very prominent young man in the entertainment world, addressing a tremendous gathering in California. It was during the time of the cold war, and communism and our own way of life were very much on people's minds. And he was speaking to that subject. And suddenly, though, I heard him saying, "I love my little girls more than anything——" And I said to myself, "Oh, no, don't. You can't—don't say that." But I had underestimated him. He went on: "I would rather see my little girls die now, still believing in God, than have them grow up under communism and one day die no longer believing in God."

There were thousands of young people in that audience. They came to their feet with shouts of joy. They had instantly recognized the profound truth in what he had said, with regard to the physical and the soul and what was truly important.

Yes, let us pray for the salvation of all of those who live in that totalitarian darkness—pray they will discover the joy of knowing God. But until they do, let us be aware that while they preach the supremacy of the state, declare its omnipotence over individual man, and predict its eventual domination of all peoples on the Earth, they are the focus of evil in the modern world. . . .

So, I urge you to speak out against those who would place the United States in a position of military and moral inferiority. You know, I've always believed that old Screwtape[2] reserved his best efforts for those of you in the church. So, in your discussions of the nuclear freeze proposals, I urge you to beware the temptation of pride—the temptation of blithely declaring yourselves above it all and label both sides equally at fault, to ignore the facts of history and the aggressive impulses of an evil empire, to simply call the arms race a giant misunderstanding and thereby remove yourself from the struggle between right and wrong and good and evil.

I ask you to resist the attempts of those who would have you withhold your support for our efforts, this administration's efforts, to keep America strong and free, while we negotiate real and verifiable reductions in the world's nuclear arsenals and one day, with God's help, their total elimination.

While America's military strength is important, let me add here that I've always maintained that the struggle now going on for the world will never be decided by bombs or rockets, by armies or military might. The

[1]Pat Boone, famous actor and singer.
[2]Literary reference to one of the Devil's minions.

real crisis we face today is a spiritual one; at root, it is a test of moral will and faith. . . .

I believe we shall rise to the challenge. I believe that communism is another sad, bizarre chapter in human history whose last pages even now are being written. I believe this because the source of our strength in the quest for human freedom is not material, but spiritual. And because it knows no limitation, it must terrify and ultimately triumph over those who would enslave their fellow man. For in the words of Isaiah: "He giveth power to the faint; and to them that have no might He increased strength. . . . But they that wait upon the Lord shall renew their strength; they shall mount up with wings as eagles; they shall run, and not be weary."

Yes, change your world. One of our Founding Fathers, Thomas Paine, said, "We have it within our power to begin the world over again." We can do it, doing together what no one church could do by itself.

26

RONALD REAGAN

Remarks at an Ecumenical Prayer Breakfast in Dallas, Texas

August 23, 1984

In this characteristic speech given during Ronald Reagan's 1984 presidential reelection campaign, the president explains how religion should function in the public sphere and demonstrates why he was so popular among the Religious Right.

It's wonderful to be here this morning. The past few days have been pretty busy for all of us, but I've wanted to be with you today to share some of my own thoughts.

Ronald Reagan, "Remarks at an Ecumenical Prayer Breakfast in Dallas, Texas," August 23, 1984, www.presidency.ucsb.edu/ws/index.php?pid=40282&st=prayer+breakfast&st1=#ixzz1MokmDpI4.

These past few weeks it seems that we've all been hearing a lot of talk about religion and its role in politics, religion and its place in the political life of the Nation. . . .

I believe that faith and religion play a critical role in the political life of our nation—and always has—and that the church—and by that I mean all churches, all denominations—has had a strong influence on the state. And this has worked to our benefit as a nation.

Those who created our country—the Founding Fathers and Mothers—understood that there is a divine order which transcends the human order. They saw the state, in fact, as a form of moral order and felt that the bedrock of moral order is religion.

The Mayflower Compact began with the words, "In the name of God, amen." The Declaration of Independence appeals to "Nature's God" and the "Creator" and "the Supreme Judge of the world." Congress was given a chaplain, and the oaths of office are oaths before God.

James Madison in the Federalist Papers admitted that in the creation of our Republic he perceived the hand of the Almighty. John Jay, the first Chief Justice of the Supreme Court, warned that we must never forget the God from whom our blessings flowed. . . .

I believe that George Washington knew the City of Man cannot survive without the City of God, that the Visible City will perish without the Invisible City.

Religion played not only a strong role in our national life, it played a positive role. The abolitionist movement was at heart a moral and religious movement; so was the modern civil rights struggle. And throughout this time, the state was tolerant of religious belief, expression, and practice. Society, too, was tolerant.

But in the 1960's this began to change. We began to make great steps toward secularizing our nation and removing religion from its honored place.

In 1962 the Supreme Court in the New York prayer case banned the compulsory saying of prayers. In 1963 the Court banned the reading of the Bible in our public schools. From that point on, the courts pushed the meaning of the ruling ever outward, so that now our children are not allowed voluntary prayer. We even had to pass a law—we passed a special law in the Congress just a few weeks ago to allow student prayer groups the same access to schoolrooms after classes that a young Marxist society, for example, would already enjoy with no opposition.

The 1962 decision opened the way to a flood of similar suits. Once religion had been made vulnerable, a series of assaults were made in one court after another, on one issue after another. Cases were started to argue against tax-exempt status for churches. Suits were brought to abolish the words "under God" from the Pledge of Allegiance and to remove "In God We Trust" from public documents and from our currency.

Today there are those who are fighting to make sure voluntary prayer is not returned to the classrooms. And the frustrating thing for the great majority of Americans who support and understand the special importance of religion in the national life—the frustrating thing is that those who are attacking religion claim they are doing it in the name of tolerance, freedom, and open-mindedness. Question: Isn't the real truth that they are intolerant of religion? [Applause] They refuse to tolerate its importance in our lives.

If all the children of our country studied together all of the many religions in our country, wouldn't they learn greater tolerance of each other's beliefs? If children prayed together, would they not understand what they have in common, and would this not, indeed, bring them closer, and is this not to be desired? So, I submit to you that those who claim to be fighting for tolerance on this issue may not be tolerant at all.

When John Kennedy was running for President in 1960, he said that his church would not dictate his Presidency any more than he would speak for his church. Just so, and proper. But John Kennedy was speaking in an America in which the role of religion—and by that I mean the role of all churches—was secure. Abortion was not a political issue. Prayer was not a political issue. The right of church schools to operate was not a political issue. And it was broadly acknowledged that religious leaders had a right and a duty to speak out on the issues of the day. They held a place of respect, and a politician who spoke to or of them with a lack of respect would not long survive in the political arena.

It was acknowledged then that religion held a special place, occupied a special territory in the hearts of the citizenry. The climate has changed greatly since then. And since it has, it logically follows that religion needs defenders against those who care only for the interests of the state.

There are, these days, many questions on which religious leaders are obliged to offer their moral and theological guidance, and such guidance is a good and necessary thing. To know how a church and its members feel on a public issue expands the parameters of debate. It does not narrow the debate; it expands it.

The truth is, politics and morality are inseparable. And as morality's foundation is religion, religion and politics are necessarily related. We need religion as a guide. We need it because we are imperfect, and our government needs the church, because only those humble enough to admit they're sinners can bring to democracy the tolerance it requires in order to survive.

A state is nothing more than a reflection of its citizens; the more decent the citizens, the more decent the state. If you practice a religion, whether you're Catholic, Protestant, Jewish, or guided by some other faith, then your private life will be influenced by a sense of moral obligation, and so, too, will your public life. One affects the other. The churches of America do not exist by the grace of the state; the churches of America are not mere citizens of the state. The churches of America exist apart; they have their own vantage point, their own authority. Religion is its own realm; it makes its own claims.

We establish no religion in this country, nor will we ever. We command no worship. We mandate no belief. But we poison our society when we remove its theological underpinnings. We court corruption when we leave it bereft of belief. All are free to believe or not believe; all are free to practice a faith or not. But those who believe must be free to speak of and act on their belief, to apply moral teaching to public questions.

I submit to you that the tolerant society is open to and encouraging of all religions. And this does not weaken us; it strengthens us, it makes us strong. You know, if we look back through history to all those great civilizations, those great nations that rose up to even world dominance and then deteriorated, declined, and fell, we find they all had one thing in common. One of the significant forerunners of their fall was their turning away from their God or gods.

Without God, there is no virtue, because there's no prompting of the conscience. Without God, we're mired in the material, that flat world that tells us only what the senses perceive. Without God, there is a coarsening of the society. And without God, democracy will not and cannot long endure. If we ever forget that we're one nation under God, then we will be a nation gone under.

If I could just make a personal statement of my own—in these 3½ years I have understood and known better than ever before the words of Lincoln, when he said that he would be the greatest fool on this footstool called Earth if he ever thought that for one moment he could perform the duties of that office without help from One who is stronger than all.

I thank you, thank you for inviting us here today. Thank you for your kindness and your patience. May God keep you, and may we, all of us, keep God. Thank you.

27

LARRY FLYNT

A Pornographer's Eulogy for Jerry Falwell

May 20, 2007

Although the Religious Right continues to be a major force in American politics, one of its most controversial leaders—Jerry Falwell—died in 2007. Hustler magazine publisher Larry Flynt provides a glimpse into the "real" Falwell in this eulogy.

The first time the Rev. Jerry Falwell put his hands on me, I was stunned. Not only had we been archenemies for 15 years, his beliefs and mine traveling in different solar systems, and not only had he sued me for $50 million (a case I lost repeatedly yet eventually won in the Supreme Court), but now he was hugging me in front of millions on the Larry King show.

It was 1997. My autobiography, "An Unseemly Man," had just been published, describing my life as a publisher of pornography. The film "The People vs. Larry Flynt" had recently come out, and the country was well aware of the battle that Falwell and I had fought: a battle that had changed the laws governing what the American public can see and hear in the media and that had dramatically strengthened our right to free speech.

King was conducting the interview. It was the first time since the infamous 1988 trial that the reverend and I had been in the same room together, and the thought of even breathing the same air with him made me sick. I disagreed with Falwell (who died last week) on absolutely everything he preached, and he looked at me as symbolic of all the social ills that a society can possibly have. But I'd do anything to sell the book and the film, and Falwell would do anything to preach, so King's audience of 8 million viewers was all the incentive either of us needed to bring us together.

Larry Flynt, "My Friend, Jerry Falwell," *Los Angeles Times*, May 20, 2007, www .latimes.com/news/opinion/commentary/la-op-flynt20may20,0,2751741.story.

But let's start at the beginning and flash back to the late 1970s, when the battle between Falwell, the leader of the Moral Majority, and I first began. I was publishing Hustler magazine, which most people know has been pushing the envelope of taste from the very beginning, and Falwell was blasting me every chance he had. He would talk about how I was a slime dealer responsible for the decay of all morals. He called me every terrible name he could think of—names as bad, in my opinion, as any language used in my magazine.

After several years of listening to him bash me and reading his insults, I decided it was time to start poking some fun at him. So we ran a parody ad in Hustler—a takeoff on the then-current Campari ads in which people were interviewed describing "their first time." In the ads, it ultimately became clear that the interviewees were describing their first time sipping Campari. But not in our parody. We had Falwell describing his "first time" as having been with his mother, "drunk off our God-fearing asses," in an outhouse.

Apparently, the reverend didn't find the joke funny. He sued us for libel in federal court in Virginia, claiming that the magazine had inflicted emotional stress on him. It was a long and tedious fight, beginning in 1983 and ending in 1988, but Hustler Magazine Inc. vs. Jerry Falwell was without question my most important battle.

We lost in our initial jury trial, and we lost again in federal appeals court. After spending a fortune, everyone's advice to me was to just settle the case and be done, but I wasn't listening; I wasn't about to pay Falwell $200,000 for hurting his feelings or, as his lawyers called it, "intentional infliction of emotional distress." We appealed to the U.S. 4th Circuit Court of Appeals, and I lost for a third time.

Everyone was certain this was the end. We never thought the U.S. Supreme Court would agree to hear the case. But it did, and though I felt doomed throughout the trial and was convinced that I was going to lose, we never gave up. As we had moved up the judicial ladder, this case had become much more than just a personal battle between a pornographer and a preacher, because the 1st Amendment was so much at the heart of the case.

To my amazement, we won. It wasn't until after I won the case and read the justices' unanimous decision in my favor that I realized fully the significance of what had happened. The justices held that a parody of a public figure was protected under the 1st Amendment even if it was outrageous, even if it was "doubtless gross and repugnant," as they put it, and even if it was designed to inflict emotional distress. In a unanimous decision—written by, of all people, Chief Justice William H.

Rehnquist—the court reasoned that if it supported Falwell's lower-court victory, no one would ever have to prove something was false and libelous to win a judgment. All anyone would have to prove is that "he upset me" or "she made me feel bad." The lawsuits would be endless, and that would be the end of free speech.

Everyone was shocked at our victory—and no one more so than Falwell, who on the day of the decision called me a "sleaze merchant" hiding behind the 1st Amendment. Still, over time, Falwell was forced to publicly come to grips with the reality that this is America, where you can make fun of anyone you want. That hadn't been absolutely clear before our case, but now it's being taught in law schools all over the country, and our case is being hailed as one of the most important free-speech cases of the 20th century.

No wonder that when he started hugging me and smooching me on television 10 years later, I was a bit confused. I hadn't seen him since we'd been in court together, and that night I didn't see him until I came out on the stage. I was expecting (and looking for) a fight, but instead he was putting his hands all over me. I remember thinking, "I spent $3 million taking that case to the Supreme Court, and now this guy wants to put his hand on my leg?"

Soon after that episode, I was in my office in Beverly Hills, and out of nowhere my secretary buzzes me, saying, "Jerry Falwell is here to see you." I was shocked, but I said, "Send him in." We talked for two hours, with the latest issues of Hustler neatly stacked on my desk in front of him. He suggested that we go around the country debating, and I agreed. We went to colleges, debating moral issues and 1st Amendment issues—what's "proper," what's not and why.

In the years that followed and up until his death, he'd come to see me every time he was in California. We'd have interesting philosophical conversations. We'd exchange personal Christmas cards. He'd show me pictures of his grandchildren. I was with him in Florida once when he complained about his health and his weight, so I suggested that he go on a diet that had worked for me. I faxed a copy to his wife when I got back home.

The truth is, the reverend and I had a lot in common. He was from Virginia, and I was from Kentucky. His father had been a bootlegger, and I had been one too in my 20s before I went into the Navy. We steered our conversations away from politics, but religion was within bounds. He wanted to save me and was determined to get me out of "the business."

My mother always told me that no matter how repugnant you find a person, when you meet them face to face you will always find something about them to like. The more I got to know Falwell, the more I began to see that his public portrayals were caricatures of himself. There was a dichotomy between the real Falwell and the one he showed the public.

He was definitely selling brimstone religion and would do anything to add another member to his mailing list. But in the end, I knew what he was selling, and he knew what I was selling, and we found a way to communicate.

I always kicked his ass about his crazy ideas and the things he said. Every time I'd call him, I'd get put right through, and he'd let me berate him about his views. When he was getting blasted for his ridiculous homophobic comments after he wrote his "Tinky Winky" article cautioning parents that the purple Teletubby character was in fact gay, I called him in Florida and yelled at him to "leave the Tinky Winkies alone."

When he referred to Ellen Degeneres in print as Ellen "Degenerate," I called him and said, "What are you doing? You don't need to poison the whole lake with your venom." I could hear him mumbling out of the side of his mouth, "These lesbians just drive me crazy." I'm sure I never changed his mind about anything, just as he never changed mine.

I'll never admire him for his views or his opinions. To this day, I'm not sure if his television embrace was meant to mend fences, to show himself to the public as a generous and forgiving preacher or merely to make me uneasy, but the ultimate result was one I never expected and was just as shocking a turn to me as was winning that famous Supreme Court case: We became friends.

A Chronology of the Religious Right (1925–2007)

1925 *Scopes* Monkey Trial is held in Dayton, Tennessee.

1933 Jerry Falwell is born.

1941 American Council of Christian Churches is founded by Carl McIntire.

1942 The National Association of Evangelicals is organized.

1949 Billy Graham's Los Angeles revival garners national acclaim.

1954 "Under God" is added to the American Pledge of Allegiance.

1956 Congress makes "In God We Trust" the national motto.

Falwell founds the Thomas Road Baptist Church.

1960 Pat Robertson incorporates what soon becomes the first Christian television station.

1962 The Supreme Court rules in *Engel v. Vitale* that mandated school prayer is unconstitutional.

Cuban missile crisis occurs.

1963 The Supreme Court rules in *Abington School District v. Schempp* that mandated school Bible reading is unconstitutional.

Women's rights activist Betty Friedan publishes *The Feminine Mystique*.

President John F. Kennedy is assassinated.

1964 Congress passes the Civil Rights Act, outlawing discrimination.

Educators organize the Sexuality Information and Education Council of the United States (SIECUS).

Democrat Lyndon B. Johnson is elected president.

1965 Civil rights activists including Martin Luther King Jr. march in Selma, Alabama.

Congress passes the Voting Rights Act, ensuring voting rights for African Americans.

1968   Republican Richard M. Nixon is elected president.

1970   Tim LaHaye and Henry Morris found the Institute for Creation Research.

Years of student rebellions against the Vietnam War culminate in the shooting deaths of students at Kent State University and Jackson State University.

The Internal Revenue Service informs Christian school Bob Jones University that its tax-exempt status is being revoked because it practices racial discrimination.

1971   Jerry Falwell founds Liberty University.

1972   Congress passes an Equal Rights Amendment (ERA) to the Constitution, which, if ratified, would guarantee equal rights for all citizens regardless of sex.

Phyllis Schlafly organizes a grassroots campaign against the ERA.

1973   The Supreme Court expands abortion rights in *Roe v. Wade*.

The SEC investigates Falwell's ministries.

Ronald Sider founds Evangelicals for Social Action.

Anti-abortion activists organize the National Right to Life Committee.

1974   Richard Nixon resigns amid Watergate scandal; Vice President Gerald Ford is sworn in as president.

1976   *Newsweek* identifies 1976 as the Year of the Evangelical.

Democrat Jimmy Carter, a born-again Christian, is elected president.

1977   James Dobson founds Focus on the Family.

Anita Bryant launches a campaign against the expansion of homosexual rights.

1979   Paul Weyrich, Richard Viguerie, and Jerry Falwell organize the Moral Majority.

1980   Republican Ronald Reagan is elected president.

1982   Ronald Reagan proposes a constitutional amendment legalizing school prayer.

1983   The Supreme Court rules against Bob Jones University, denying tax-exempt status to schools that practice discrimination.

James Dobson founds the Family Research Council.

1984   Ronald Reagan is reelected president.

1986   Randall Terry organizes an anti-abortion group that soon becomes Operation Rescue.

1987   Jerry Falwell retires from the Moral Majority.

1988   Pat Robertson seeks the Republican nomination for president.
           Republican George H. W. Bush is elected president.

1989   Pat Robertson and Ralph Reed found the Christian Coalition.

1992,
1996   Democrat Bill Clinton is elected president.

2000,
2004   Republican George W. Bush is elected president.

2007   Jerry Falwell dies.

Questions for Consideration

1. What are the characteristics of American evangelicalism?
2. How was evangelicalism expressed in Falwell's life and publications?
3. What issues and events drove Falwell and other conservative Christians to new forms of political activism in the second half of the twentieth century?
4. How would you define the Religious Right?
5. Was or is there a Religious Left?
6. What tactics did conservative Christians such as Falwell employ to shape American politics and culture?
7. What attracted American evangelicals to the Republican Party?
8. In what ways did Ronald Reagan make use of religion during his presidency?
9. How might we assess Jerry Falwell's impact, along with that of the Religious Right more generally, on American culture and politics?
10. In what ways are religious activists still influencing American politics?

Selected Bibliography

Balmer, Randall. *Mine Eyes Have Seen the Glory: A Journey into the Evangelical Subculture in America.* New York: Oxford University Press, 2000.
————. *Thy Kingdom Come: How the Religious Right Distorts the Faith and Threatens America, an Evangelical's Lament.* New York: Basic Books, 2006.
Bendroth, Margaret Lamberts. *Fundamentalism and Gender, 1875 to the Present.* New Haven, Conn.: Yale University Press, 1993.
Bivins, Jason. *The Fracture of Good Order: Christian Antiliberalism and the Challenge to American Politics.* Chapel Hill: University of North Carolina Press, 2003.
————. *Religion of Fear: The Politics of Horror in Conservative Evangelicalism.* New York: Oxford University Press, 2008.
Blum, Edward J. *Reforging the White Republic: Race, Religion, and American Nationalism, 1865–1898.* Baton Rouge: Louisiana State University Press, 2005.
Boyer, Paul S. *When Time Shall Be No More: Prophecy Belief in Modern American Culture.* Cambridge, Mass.: Belknap Press of Harvard University Press, 1992.
Carpenter, Joel A. *Revive Us Again: The Reawakening of American Fundamentalism.* New York: Oxford University Press, 1997.
Chappell, David L. *A Stone of Hope: Prophetic Religion and the Death of Jim Crow.* Chapel Hill: University of North Carolina Press, 2004.
Crespino, Joseph. *In Search of Another Country: Mississippi and the Conservative Counterrevolution.* Princeton, N.J.: Princeton University Press, 2007.
Critchlow, Donald T. *Phyllis Schlafly and Grassroots Conservatism: A Woman's Crusade.* Princeton, N.J.: Princeton University Press, 2005.
————. *The Conservative Ascendancy: How the GOP Right Made Political History.* Cambridge, Mass.: Harvard University Press, 2007.
Dochuk, Darren. *From Bible Belt to Sunbelt: Plain-Folk Religion, Grassroots Politics, and the Rise of Evangelical Conservatism.* New York: W. W. Norton, 2011.

Frykholm, Amy Johnson. *Rapture Culture: Left Behind in Evangelical America*. New York: Oxford University Press, 2004.

Hankins, Barry. *God's Rascal: J. Frank Norris and the Beginnings of Southern Fundamentalism*. Lexington: University Press of Kentucky, 1996.

———. *Francis Schaeffer and the Shaping of Evangelical America*. Grand Rapids, Mich.: William B. Eerdmans, 2008.

Harding, Susan Friend. *The Book of Jerry Falwell: Fundamentalist Language and Politics*. Princeton, N.J.: Princeton University Press, 2000.

Heineman, Kenneth J. *God Is a Conservative: Religion, Politics, and Morality in Contemporary America*. New York: New York University Press, 2005.

Herzog, Jonathan P. *The Spiritual-Industrial Complex: America's Religious Battle against Communism in the Early Cold War*. New York: Oxford University Press, 2011.

Hunter, James Davison. *Culture Wars: The Struggle to Define America*. New York: Basic Books, 1991.

Inboden, William. *Religion and American Foreign Policy, 1945–1960: The Soul of Containment*. New York: Cambridge University Press, 2008.

Kalman, Laura. *Right Star Rising: A New Politics, 1974–1980*. New York: W. W. Norton, 2010.

Lahr, Angela M. *Millennial Dreams and Apocalyptic Nightmares: The Cold War Origins of Political Evangelicalism*. New York: Oxford University Press, 2007.

Lienesch, Michael. *Redeeming America: Piety and Politics in the New Christian Right*. Chapel Hill: University of North Carolina Press, 1993.

Marsden, George M. *Reforming Fundamentalism: Fuller Seminary and the New Evangelicalism*. Grand Rapids, Mich.: William B. Eerdmans, 1987.

———. *Fundamentalism and American Culture*. New York: Oxford University Press, 2006.

Martin, William C. *With God on Our Side: The Rise of the Religious Right in America*. New York: Broadway Books, 2005.

McGirr, Lisa. *Suburban Warriors: The Origins of the New American Right*. Princeton, N.J.: Princeton University Press, 2001.

Miller, Steven P. *Billy Graham and the Rise of the Republican South*. Philadelphia: University of Pennsylvania Press, 2009.

Moreton, Bethany. *To Serve God and Wal-Mart: The Making of Christian Free Enterprise*. Cambridge, Mass.: Harvard University Press, 2009.

Noll, Mark A. *God and Race in American Politics: A Short History*. Princeton, N.J.: Princeton University Press, 2008.

Noll, Mark A., and Luke E. Harlow. *Religion and American Politics: From the Colonial Period to the Present*. New York: Oxford University Press, 2007.

Preston, Andrew. *Sword of the Spirit, Shield of Faith: Religion in American War and Diplomacy*. New York: Alfred A. Knopf, 2012.

Ribuffo, Leo P. *The Old Christian Right: The Protestant Far Right from the Great Depression to the Cold War*. Philadelphia: Temple University Press, 1983.

Schulman, Bruce J., and Julian E. Zelizer. *Rightward Bound: Making America Conservative in the 1970s*. Cambridge, Mass.: Harvard University Press, 2008.

Sehat, David. *The Myth of American Religious Freedom*. New York: Oxford University Press, 2011.

Smillie, Dirk. *Falwell Inc.: Inside a Religious, Political, Educational, and Business Empire*. New York: St. Martin's Press, 2008.

Smith, Christian. *Christian America? What Evangelicals Really Want*. Berkeley: University of California Press, 2000.

Stephens, Randall J. *The Fire Spreads: Holiness and Pentecostalism in the American South*. Cambridge, Mass.: Harvard University Press, 2008.

Stephens, Randall J., and Karl Giberson. *The Anointed: Evangelical Truth in a Secular Age*. Cambridge, Mass.: Belknap Press of Harvard University Press, 2011.

Sutton, Matthew Avery. *Aimee Semple McPherson and the Resurrection of Christian America*. Cambridge, Mass.: Harvard University Press, 2007.

Turner, John G. *Bill Bright and Campus Crusade for Christ: The Renewal of Evangelicalism in Postwar America*. Chapel Hill: University of North Carolina Press, 2008.

Wacker, Grant. *Heaven Below: Early Pentecostals and American Culture*. Cambridge, Mass.: Harvard University Press, 2001.

Weber, Timothy. *On the Road to Armageddon: How Evangelicals Became Israel's Best Friend*. Grand Rapids, Mich.: Baker Academic, 2004.

Wilcox, Clyde. *God's Warriors: The Christian Right in Twentieth-Century America*. Baltimore: Johns Hopkins University Press, 1992.

Wilentz, Sean. *The Age of Reagan: A History, 1974–2008*. New York: Harper, 2008.

Williams, Daniel K. *God's Own Party: The Making of the Christian Right*. New York: Oxford University Press, 2010.

Winters, Michael Sean. *God's Right Hand: How Jerry Falwell Made God a Republican and Baptized the American Right*. New York: HarperOne, 2012.

Acknowledgments (continued from p. iv)

Photo, p. 9. Liberty University, Inc.

Photo, p. 23. Courtesy Ronald Reagan Library.

Photo, p. 24. © Bettmann/CORBIS.

Document 1. From Harold John Ockenga, "The 'New' Evangelism," in *Park Street Spire*, pp. 2–7; Harold John Ockenga Papers (Gordon Conwell Theological Seminary, South Hamilton, Mass.). Used by permission of Park Street Church, Boston, MA.

Document 2. "America at the Crossroads" by Billy Graham, from "Hour of Decision," © 1958 Billy Graham Evangelistic Association. Used with permission. All rights reserved.

Document 3. Hal Lindsey. Pages 2, 52–58, 135–38, 144, 181–88 from *The Late Great Planet Earth* by Hal Lindsey (Grand Rapids, Mich.: Zondervan Publishing House). Copyright © 1970 Hal Lindsey. Reprinted by permission of the author.

Document 4. "Chicago Declaration of Evangelical Social Concern" from Evangelicals for Social Action, www.evangelicalsforsocialaction.org/document.doc?id=107. Used by permission of Ronald Sider.

Document 5. Taken from *A Christian Manifesto* by Francis A. Schaeffer, © 1981, pp. 17–24, 131–33. Used by permission of Crossway, a publishing ministry of Good News Publishers, Wheaton, Ill. 60187, www.crossway.org.

Document 6. From L. Nelson Bell, "Christian Race Relations Must Be Natural—Not Forced," in *Southern Presbyterian Journal*, August 17, 1955, pp. 3–5. Reprinted with permission from the Southern Presbyterian Journal.

Document 7. Carl McIntire. Letter on Civil Rights to Lyndon B. Johnson, March 26, 1964, Carl McIntire Papers, Princeton Theological Seminary. Reprinted by permission of the Carl McIntire Family.

Document 8. From Jerry Falwell, "Ministers and Marches" (Lynchburg, Va.: Thomas Road Baptist Church). Used by permission of Thomas Road Baptist Church.

Document 10. From Clarence Hilliard, "Down with the Honky Christ—Up with the Funky Jesus," in *Christianity Today*, January 30, 1976, pp. 430–32. Special thanks to the estate of the late Rev. Clarence I. Hilliard.

Document 12. Tim LaHaye. Pages ii, 1–4, 6–9, 30–31, 40–43, 45–46 from *A Christian View of Radical Sex Education* by Tim LaHaye (San Diego: Family Life Seminars). Copyright © 1969 by Tim LaHaye. Reprinted by permission of Tim LaHaye, Author, Minister, Christian Educator.

Document 13. From "Five Things We Think You Will Like about Lynchburg Christian Academy," 1975, Lynchburg Christian Academy folder, Liberty University Archives. Used by permission of Liberty Christian Academy.

Document 14. Peter Marshall and David Manuel. Pages 13–20, 22–26 from *The Light and the Glory* by Peter Marshall and David Manuel (Old Tappan, N.J.: Revell). Copyright © 1977 by Revell, a division of Baker Publishing Group. Used by permission.

Document 15. From *Dinosaurs: Those Terrible Lizards* by Duane Gish, 1977; 9, 12–13, 15–16, 56–57, 59–60. Used with permission from the publisher, Creation-Life Publishers.

Document 16. From Carl F. H. Henry, "Abortion: An Evangelical View," in *Christian Heritage*, February 1971, pp. 22–25. Courtesy of the Family of Carl F. H. Henry.

Document 18. From "When the Homoscxuals Burn the Holy Bible in Public . . . How Can I Stand By Silently." Reprinted by permission of Anita Bryant Ministries, copyright © 1977.

Document 19. Jerry Falwell, Pages 67, 70–72 from *How You Can Help Clean Up America* (Lynchburg, Va.: Liberty Publishing Company). Copyright © 1978 by Liberty Publishing Company. Used by permission of Thomas Road Baptist Church.

Document 20. Marabel Morgan. Pages 15, 17, 19, 22–23, 26–27, 57–58, 68–70, 91–95, 183–84 from *The Total Woman* by Marabel Morgan (Old Tappan, N.J.: Revell). Copyright © 1973 by Marabel Morgan. Used by permission of Marabel Morgan, author, *The Total Woman.*

Document 21. "Dialogue with Phyllis Schlafly," *Moody Monthly* (November 1978), 44–49. Reprinted by permission of Moody Publishers.

Document 22. Pat Robertson, "Action Plan for the 1980s," from Records of National Religious Broadcasters, file 6, box 29, collection 309; Billy Graham Center Archives, Wheaton, Ill. Reprinted by permission of Pat Robertson.

Document 23. From *Listen, America!* by Jerry Falwell, copyright © 1980 by Jerry Falwell. Used by permission of Doubleday, a division of Random House, Inc.

Document 27. Larry Flynt, "My Friend, Jerry Falwell," *Los Angeles Times,* May 20, 2007. Copyright © 2007 by Larry Flynt. Reprinted by permission of Larry Flynt.

Index